BASICS

ADVERTISING

03

Nik Mahon

Ethical: aware-
ness/
reflect-
ion/
debate

ava
academia

An AVA Book

Published by AVA Publishing SA
Rue des Fontenailles 16
Case Postale
1000 Lausanne 6
Switzerland
Tel: +41 786 005 109
Email: enquiries@avabooks.com

Distributed by Thames & Hudson (ex-North America)
181a High Holborn
London WC1V 7QX
United Kingdom
Tel: +44 20 7845 5000
Fax: +44 20 7845 5055
Email: sales@thameshudson.co.uk
www.thamesandhudson.com

Distributed in the USA & Canada by:
Ingram Publisher Services Inc.
1 Ingram Blvd.
La Vergne TN 37086
USA
Tel: +1 866 400 5351
Fax: +1 800 838 1149
Email: customer.service@ingrampublisherservices.com

English Language Support Office
AVA Publishing (UK) Ltd.
Tel: +44 1903 204 455
Email: enquiries@avabooks.com

ISBN 978-2-940411-50-4

Library of Congress Cataloging-in-Publication Data
Mahon, Nik.
Basics Advertising 03: Ideation/Nik Mahon p. cm.
Includes bibliographical references and index.
ISBN: 9782940411504 (pbk.:alk.paper)
eISBN: 9782940447190
1.Advertising.2.Advertising campaigns.
HF5837 .M356 2011

10 9 8 7 6 5 4 3 2 1

Design by David Shaw

Production by AVA Book Production Pte. Ltd., Singapore
Tel: +65 6334 8173
Fax: +65 6259 9830
Email: production@avabooks.com.sg

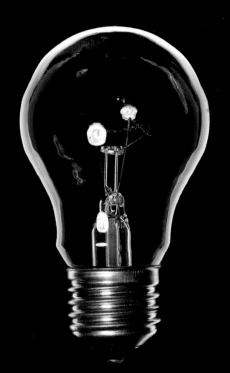

Table of contents

4

Having a great idea is difficult enough. Having great ideas repeatedly, and on a regular basis, is the real creative challenge

At the heart of every successful advertising campaign is a central proposition that binds each of the adverts in that campaign together in a cohesive and fully integrated manner. Expressing this proposition in an original, novel, imaginative, memorable, yet relevant fashion is the tricky bit – particularly when it seems that all the best ideas have already been used. Having a great idea is difficult enough. Having great ideas repeatedly, and on a regular basis, is the real creative challenge. On many occasions, you may simply feel that you're out of fresh ideas, or have come up against a creative block. This is where *Ideation* can help you break through to find creative solutions.

The book begins by looking at the process of idea generation (ideation) in broad terms; establishing the key principles that are involved, together with a look at what stops us having ideas, and how to get around or avoid those obstacles. It proceeds to outline various tools and specific techniques for stimulating creativity and having ideas, as well as a range of different styles of approach and execution available to the creative team.

Throughout the book, various case studies illustrate the content and provide some valuable insights into the development of creative concepts. Student exercises promote a deeper understanding of the ideation process and help the reader to hone his or her ideation skills.

1

What *is* ideation?

Understanding the process of ideation is central to creative fluency. Key principles include the need to suspend premature judgement of ideas, the need for wild or provocative ideas, and the tenet that quantity eventually yields quality. Mind sets, logic, adequacy of resources, risk aversion and routine working practices or problem-solving approaches are just some of the things that can channel our thinking in too narrow a direction, preventing us from making creative breakthroughs.

2

Breaking through to ideas

Breaking through the creative blocks begins with the practices that we adopt for tackling creative problems. The capacity to change habits, break routine, challenge well-worn procedures, and to experiment and see things differently, is characteristic of the greatest creative thinkers. The manner in which the creative team interact with each other to re-interpret and interrogate the brief is fundamental to the ideation process.

3

Using creative tools to generate ideas

When you're up against a tight deadline and solutions aren't forthcoming, specific methods and techniques for stimulating creativity and liberating fresh ideas can be useful tools to be equipped with. Even at the outset of the creative process, using some of the techniques described here will prompt lateral thinking and stimulate ideas, resulting in a more productive process overall.

4

Executing creative ideas successfully

Once you've got a great idea, the way you execute that idea needs to be determined. There are a wide variety of approaches to choose from, and in many cases these are inextricably linked to, or part of, the creative idea itself. This chapter takes a look at some of the most common approaches, from reframing, humour, shock advertising and the use of sex, to demonstrations, tests, topicality and testimonials.

Ideation is the process of generating creative ideas. The term 'ideation' is a portmanteau word that combines the words 'idea' and 'generation'.

For some, it can be a natural thing that happens without conscious effort or premeditati For others, it may happen through a concerted effort and necessitate a more systematic approach involving specific techniques. Some of us feel more creative at certain times of the day or while performing certain activities; others may find certain environments or surroundings more conducive to creativity.

One thing about ideation is common to us all: we can never know if or when that 'eureka moment' will occur. In some creative fields, it's okay to simply wait however long it take for inspiration. In advertising, where there is always a deadlin tomorrow, it's necessary to take proactive measures to gain inspiration and generate creative solutions.

no magic formula
hod or approach
 ideas and finding
ions, there are
a few general
deation that you
k up. Gaining a
nding of these
gether with
e knowledge of
al process
nking operates,
tly increase your
ving great ideas
t you need to tackle
blem or brief.

Divergent and convergent thinking

To help you get started, think of the route that you need to take from a creative problem to a creative solution as a *journey*. This is an analogy that we'll revisit on several occasions throughout this book.

The quickest and safest route to a creative solution is the direct, well-trodden pathway that can sometimes lead to the first idea that pops into your head, or at other times to a solution that's very similar to previous solutions that you may have arrived at. Using the same conventional linear approach each time that you're faced with a creative advertising brief will undoubtedly guarantee that you'll reach a solution, but it's highly unlikely that this solution will break any new creative ground and be noticeably different from past ideas that you've had.

Divergent thinking

The best way to find new ideas is to start with fresh ways of approaching the problem that you're confronted with; this requires the use of divergent thinking. Divergent thinking is a term used to describe the process of looking in different directions for alternative ideas (or to use a well-worn and hackneyed phrase, of 'thinking outside the box').

Divergent thinking represents the essence of creativity. It leads us to ideas and sometimes to random thoughts that are often so far from the conventional or logical way that we would normally approach the brief that it can be
easy to get carried away with an exciting idea

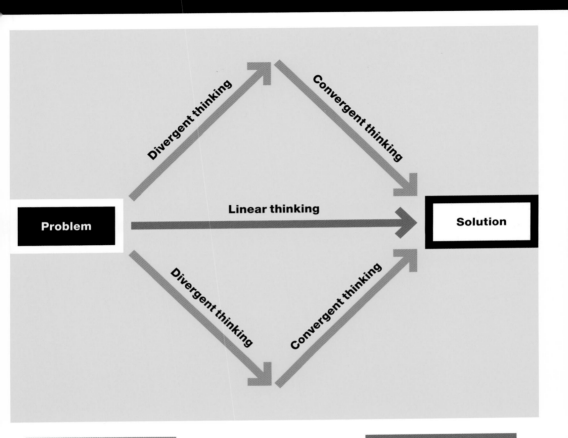

Convergent thinking

Convergent thinking refers to when we have to refocus on the creative problem and evaluate the thoughts and ideas that have been generated through divergent thinking in order to see if any of them can be successfully used or adapted to provide adequate solutions that are both highly original and relevant to the brief.

From problem to solution

Divergent thinking is the creative phase of the ideation process that involves exploring alternative lateral ideas; whereas convergent thinking brings us back on track by evaluating those ideas in terms of the objectives outlined in the creative brief and filtering through those ideas that may provide viable creative solutions. In some fields of business, divergent/convergent thinking is sometimes referred to as 'loose/tight thinking'.

The principles of ideation

Preparation, incubation, illumination and verification

The creative process broadly involves four sequential phases or stages; preparation, incubation, illumination and verification, which we shall explore in more detail below.

Preparation

The preparation stage includes all the effort that is invested in the initial part of the process. For advertising creatives, this will involve everything from the creative briefing through to subsequent research or fact-finding measures undertaken to discover more about the product, brand or service to be advertised. It will also include any initial brainstorming sessions or first thoughts regarding the brief and may result in the creation of some initial ideas.

Directly sampling or experiencing the product or service by talking to those who make it, sell it, buy it or use it can also enable you to discover interesting things about it and so trigger an original concept for a whole campaign. Surrounding yourself with articles and objects associated with the product while it's in front of you can also liberate new ideas and keep your brain working on the creative problem, even when you're not really thinking about it.

Preparation also includes the kind of activities that you might routinely engage in but that may not be specifically related to the problem at hand. The films you watch, the books you read, the music you listen to, the art galleries you visit and the people you meet are just a few of the everyday influences that inform how you perceive the world around you and that will influence how you approach the tasks you are presented with.

Essentially, the preparation stage is about priming yourself for inspiration. It's important to remember that without any input, there can be no output. Creativity needs to be fed, and absorbing information from an eclectic range of sources is key to finding a solution that's both unique and unexpected.

Incubation

Once you've done the preparation work, it's time to step back from the brief and simply allow ideas to gestate. This is particularly true if you've spent a long time trying hard to have an idea. The best ideas rarely happen whilst you're staring at a blank page of layout paper and it's more often the case that the harder you try, the more difficult it becomes to have an idea – so just relax and do something else. Go for a jog, take a bath, read the newspaper, have a coffee, or simply work on another project for a while. In many cases, you'll find that you'll have your best ideas for project A whilst you're working on project B (and vice versa). Crucially, taking a break from the problem gives you some creative space and allows you to return to it with fresh eyes.

The best ideas rarely happen whilst you're staring at a blank page of layout paper and it's more often the case that the harder you try, the more difficult it becomes to have an idea – so just relax and do something else

Illumination

The illumination stage is the point at which an idea is realized – more commonly referred to as the moment of inspiration. The Romantic poet Shelley once likened this moment to embers glowing brightly on a fire seconds before they burn out to become ash. Ideas often surface unexpectedly and rarely on schedule. We may become aware of them only briefly before they once again get submerged in the noise of our daily thoughts and routines. It's important to have a means of capturing and recording those ideas when they surface in order to fully explore their potential as solutions to the creative problem.

Verification

The final stage is verification of the idea. This is where divergent thinking switches to convergent thinking and we evaluate the quality and appropriateness of the idea against the criteria of the brief.

Don't judge your ideas too early

It's important that you don't judge your ideas too prematurely. We're all prone to quickly dismissing ideas that may suddenly come to mind purely on the basis that they might initially seem a bit crazy or not altogether that relevant. The rule here is to capture *every* idea as it surfaces, not just the ones that seem to provide obvious solutions. There'll be a chance to assess their worth later on during the verification stage of the process, but at the outset it's a case of recording every idea as it immediately occurs. You're likely to find that the stranger ideas (and those that may seem more remote from the brief itself) are the ones likely to provide more unexpected and lateral solutions.

The key to divergent thinking is not to pore too long or hard over each idea as you have it, or to dwell upon whether it's a good or a bad idea. The point of divergent thinking is precisely that you are licensed to think beyond the boundaries of logic and reasoning. It's also important to get every idea you have out of your head and down onto paper as quickly as possible.

If you really do have a 'bad' idea, the chances are that it will keep coming back to haunt you throughout the duration of the project. One sure way to 'exorcise' that idea is to capture it and to then later test it out with all your other ideas. Explore different ways by which it could actually provide you with a solution – and then if it really does turn out to be a genuinely bad idea you can simply choose to abandon it.

The principles of ideation

Big ideas
Some of the best creative solutions are often the simplest. This campaign for Lego features dramatic larger-than-life images of the iconic children's building bricks in different settings to represent something that's yet to be built; a fire engine, a plane or a train.
Advertising Agency:
Saatchi & Saatchi Singapore
Client: Lego
Creative Director: Andy Greenaway
Art Director: Stuart Harricks
Copywriter: Roger Makak
Photographer: Dean Zillwood, IDC

CENTRAL FIRE STATION

Build it. **LEGO**

The principles of ideation

> **The real beauty of wild ideas is in their capacity to serve as springboards for lateral ideas**

Have wild 'springboard' ideas

Divergent thinking tends to generate a large quantity of ideas that may, at first sight, either appear to have little relevance to the problem you are working on, or to present a range of solutions that are too radical or unusable for a variety of other reasons. However it is those kinds of ideas that can prove to be the most valuable, as they ultimately force you to approach the problem from a completely different, unexpected direction and require you to look for new connections in order to find a link between your idea and the brief.

The real beauty of wild ideas is in their capacity to serve as springboards for lateral ideas. In its raw state, a wild idea may be very radically different to anything that's been used before, but may at the same time remain inappropriate as an immediate solution to the brief.

For example, let's imagine for a moment that you're creating a new campaign encouraging people to visit Wales for a holiday, and the brief requires you to tell people all about the exciting things that they can see or do there. One radical idea that you might have is to challenge the proposition that there *is* a lot to see or do in Wales and instead choose to tell people that there's absolutely nothing to see or do there!

Of course, presenting this idea to the client would likely be the fastest way to lose the account. So instead treat it as a springboard idea. Ask yourself: why would you tell people that there's nothing to see or do in Wales? For instance, perhaps you could propose that the Welsh want to keep what the country has to offer all to themselves! Suddenly, you have an interesting approach to the campaign, based on the idea that '...there's a lot of great things to see or do there... but it's our secret and we're keeping it that way'.

So now you can see how those apparently 'crazy' ideas might importantly act as a springboard to real advertising solutions, and also why it's very important not to judge your ideas too early on in the process.

Crazy ideas can sell

Saxsofunny are a sound production company based in São Paulo, Brazil. To convey the message that the company can produce any type of sound that their clients desire, they created crazily shaped cases for imaginary musical instruments and sent them out to key creative people in the radio and TV departments of leading agencies in Brazil. In the immediate period that followed, their business increased by 10 per cent in comparison to the same period in the previous year.

Advertising Agency: DDB Brasil
Client: Saxsofunny
Creative Directors: Sergio Valente, Marcelo Reis, Guilherme Jahara, Cassiano Saldanha
Art Director: Max Geraldo
Copywriter: Arício Fortes
Photographer: Marcel Valvassori
Graphic Producer: Edson Harada
Client: Zezinho Mutarelli

IMAGINARY MUSICAL INSTRUMENTS

BACKGROUND: There are more than 20 good sound production companies in São Paulo. It is a very competitive market and Saxsofunny needed to stand out and be remembered by agencies when they were producing campaigns. **IDEA:** To produce cases holding imaginary musical instruments, conveying the message that the company plays all the sounds the target might need. The cases were sent to key people in the creative department of leading agencies in São Paulo and other parts of Brazil. Inside the case there was a pen drive containing the sound production company's recent reel.

SAXSOFUNNY
Sound Production Company

WE PLAY THE SOUND YOU NEED.   **SAXSOFUNNY**

View of the open box containing a pen drive with the sound production company's reel.

The principles of ideation

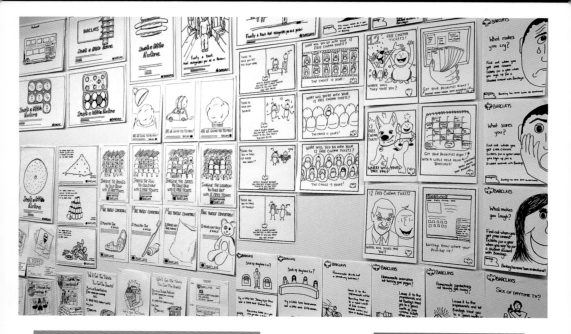

Quantity equals quality

There's no doubt that the more ideas you generate, the greater the number of really good ideas that you'll have amongst them. It could be the case that you need a hundred or so ideas before you really find one that ticks all the boxes, which is highly original, unexpected and memorable, yet relevant to the product and the brand message in a way that's campaignable across a variety of different media. This is no easy task and the ability to have not just one, but several ideas that meet the brief in this way rests on your creative fluency and your capacity to move on from one idea to the next. If you start assessing each idea as it crops up, you'll never get past first base.

Quantity equals quality

Having not one, but a hundred and one ideas for each brief is guaranteed to result in a greater level of creativity and originality.

One of the most important principles of ideation is to question everything

Keep asking questions

One of the most important principles of ideation is to question everything. Challenging things that you may be automatically assuming about the problem is key to lateral thinking and the basis of many techniques covered in this book. As children we're really good at asking lots of questions, often to the point of annoying everyone else.

By asking questions, we can open up new opportunities and discover alternative solutions. It's no wonder that small children are more creative than most adults – they just keep asking questions. It seems that as we grow up, we lose our capacity for creative enquiry and we appear content to accept most things that we are confronted with at face value. To see beyond the most obvious solutions, we need to think like a child again!

Try new combinations

Some may argue that there's no such thing as an original advertising idea anymore, and that everything has already been used in some form or another at some point in the past. It's also very hard to escape from a great idea that we've previously seen in order to produce something that's genuinely different and which represents a departure from everything else that's been tried and tested in the past.

One way to do this is to try combining existing ideas or concepts to create new ones. In fact, creating new combinations by putting together things that would not normally be associated with each other forms the essence of the creative process. The invention of the jet-ski, for example, relied simply on an amalgamation of the concepts which lie behind a pair of skis and a motorcycle. Try experimenting with random images, words or objects and see where it leads you. Later on in the book we'll be looking at how random stimuli can help you to generate fresh, original concepts as solutions to an advertising brief.

The principles of ideation

Combining images

The Potato Coalition of Manitoba
was established in response to a new
law lobbied into existence by a large
co-operative which was threatening
to force small local farms out of the
potato market. The advertising images
cleverly combined the image of a
potato with that of other endangered
species, the panda and turtle.
Advertising Agency: Cocoon Branding
Creative Director: Chuck Philips

MANITOBA POTATOES ARE

ENDANGERED

SAVE POTATOES.COM

Personal creative blocks

There are certain things that can block us from having ideas or finding alternative solutions. Sometimes these things are external factors outside our immediate control, but often they are personal circumstances or things that lie within our own scope to change or adapt. Being aware of these creative blocks and knowing how to break through or circumnavigate them is a key creative skill.

Right
Be unexpected
These posters for Coca-Cola break the traditional mind set of what a poster is and how it is seen in the context of a billboard.
Agency: MacLaren McCann
Art Director: Robert Kingston
Copywriters: Wade Hesson,
Nancy Crirni, Lauren McCrindle
Creative Directors:
Sean Davison, Andy Manson
Photographer:
Frank Hoedl, Westside Studios

Mind sets

One of the most significant blocks to creativity is something that is commonly referred to as a 'mind set'. A mind set is something that triggers a routine pattern of thinking, which inevitably results in routine ways of approaching creative problems, which in turn generate ideas and solutions that lack originality or unexpectedness.

When we have a problem to solve, our instinct is to refer back to similar problems that we have tackled in the past, and to then adopt the same approach as before in order to attempt to tackle these new problems. Our brain defaults to this method of problem solving because it recognizes it as an approach that we've already used in the past to successfully find a solution, and therefore believes that it's more likely to provide a solution again. The main flaw with this pattern of response is that whilst routine methods of problem solving may guarantee a solution, that solution is unlikely to be any different to previous solutions and is almost certain to fall short of any creative breakthrough.

Personal creative blocks

**If you become too focused
on the way that things are,
you will become less likely
to see how things could be!**

Sameness

Imagine for a moment that you have been given an advertising brief to produce a campaign for a major mobile phone brand. The first thing you may do after reading the brief is to refer back to all of the other mobile phone ads that you have seen in the past. This is only natural. Having done this, there's a good chance that your initial ideas are going to look just like every other mobile phone advert that's been seen before. There's plenty of bland advertising around and certain types of products and services are characterized by a certain sameness in the style of advertising that they tend to use and the manner in which they attempt to communicate a message. Hopefully, with a little help from some of the tools and approaches described in this book, you won't be falling into this trap too often.

Logic

Logical thinking tends to be linear and sequential in the manner by which it addresses problems. Decisions are made through an analytical and deductive process based on past experience and tested methodologies. This rational way of viewing things leaves little scope for divergent thinking or approaches that can't be fully justified. It places the burden on the problem solver to justify every direction that they choose to explore in search of a solution. However, some of the most creative ideas are generated by exploring different routes and directions that can't merely be logically explained. The best explanation that a creative might offer for having generated a specific idea might run along the lines of: 'I had a hunch it might work'; or, 'I thought it would be interesting to try it out.' It's often the case that creatives can't precisely justify or rationalize why they chose to explore a particular line of thinking – it may just come down to chance or instinct.

Fear of failure and risk aversion

Fear of failure is one of the most common things that holds us back from having great ideas. At one level, it may just be a case of worrying about whether your idea will be seen as ridiculous by others; at a more significant level, it may involve a sense of fear that implementing your idea could have disastrous or embarrassing consequences. Later on, we'll be looking at the importance and value of risk taking, but for the moment it's important to be aware that whilst risk aversion will limit the chance of failure, it will also limit the chance of any ideas arising that present a real creative leap, too.

In order to have such ideas, we must be prepared to move out of our personal comfort zone. Many clients will ask their advertising agency for fresh concepts and original ideas, but those same clients may often lose their nerve when presented with ideas that are radically different from anything else that has been done before. Brave advertising requires brave clients – and this is what distinguishes the brand leaders from the rest of the market.

Over-involvement

Whilst research, fact finding and problem familiarization are a key part of the initial preparation stage of the creative process, the more we find out about the product brand or service, the more likely it is that our thoughts will become too narrowly focused. Whilst having all this knowledge can be a good thing, it can also constrain lateral thinking. This is just one of the many contradictory phenomena that characterize creativity. Put simply: if you become too focused on the way that things are, you will become less likely to see the way that things could be!

Sometimes, we can be so involved with a project that we fail to see opportunities and alternative solutions as and when they present themselves. The closer we are to the problem the more difficult it can become to explore different routes, as our thinking becomes channelled in one direction by a series of familiar mind sets.

This is where taking a break from the problem becomes important. We've all been in the position where we've been engaged in a complex task or problem, and then have been suddenly interrupted and forced to stop what we're doing. When we're finally able to get back to the task at hand, it's often difficult to pick up from where we left off, particularly if a considerable amount of time has elapsed. When we do manage to pick up the threads, they're rarely in exactly the same order or format as before. We are forced to make new connections and (as if by magic), we also see new patterns and ideas starting to emerge that we hadn't seen earlier.

Personal creative blocks

A hunter shoots a bear

French advertising agency BUZZMAN created an online film for Tipp-Ex that depicted a series of face-to-face encounters between a hunter and a comically unrealistic bear. It begins with the hunter reaching out of the frame for the Tipp-Ex Pocket Mouse and erasing the word 'shoots' from the title, before inviting viewers to replace it with a word of their choice. More than 40 scenarios were filmed with different endings such as dances, hugs, plays football, tickles and cooks, whilst an 'explicit content' sticker was used for the more risqué suggestions! Watch the ad yourself on YouTube.
Agency: BUZZMAN
Client: Tipp-Ex

1

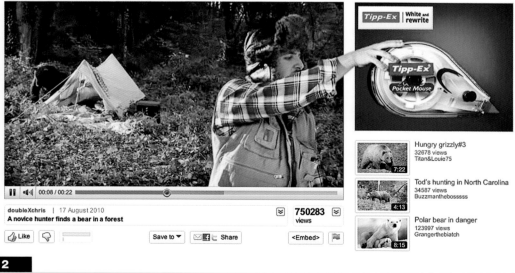

2

A hunter

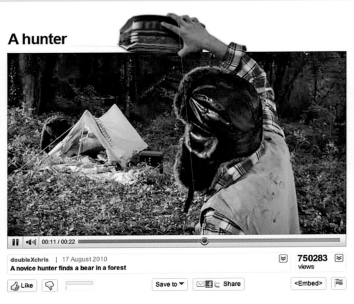

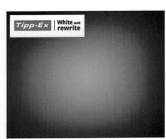

Hungry grizzly#3
32678 views
Titan&Louie75
7:22

Tod's hunting in North Carolina
34587 views
Buzzmanthebosssss
4:13

Polar bear in danger
123997 views
Grangerthebiatch
8:15

00:11 / 00:22

doubleXchris | 17 August 2010
A novice hunter finds a bear in a forest

750283 views

Like   Save to ▼   Share   <Embed>

3

A hunter hugs   a bear   ▶ Play

Join us on Facebook

00:04 / 00:25

YouTube

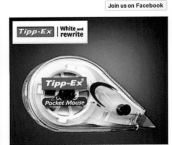

4

External blocks

There are certain external blocks that can prevent or constrain creativity that we may have very little or no control over. These can include the environment in which you work, inadequate resources, other people and adequacy (the predominant notion that 'existing solutions work fine – so why worry about looking for new ones?').

Your working environment

There's little doubt that the environment that you work in can have a significant impact on your creativity. It should ideally provide you with a creative space where you can find inspiration and where your imagination is given licence to roam. There is no single template for designing such an environment as different people will invariably need different things.

One factor, however, does seem to ring true for most people, which is that a change of environment can help to trigger creativity and re-kindle ideas when you're getting stuck. Some advertising agencies and other organizations recognize this and cater for it by providing special rooms for their employees to escape to when they need to generate fresh ideas. Such rooms can range from a spare office to specially designed theme rooms that provide a completely different environment – no prizes for guessing which is likely to provide a more fertile creative space!

It's not just the physical surroundings that go to make up your working environment. It's also the general culture and ethos of the place in which you work that can have a profound effect on your capacity to have ideas. You may be unfortunate enough to find yourself working within a culture that has little time or tolerance for any new ideas that challenge the way in which things currently operate or that may involve change. The well-worn saying, 'if it ain't broke, why fix it?' is often used to justify this kind of resistance, and in order to change such a culture, support normally has to be found at the highest level of management.

Space for creativity

The creative departments and working spaces within advertising agencies are designed to give their teams the right kind of environment in which to kindle their imagination and liberate creative ideas.

External blocks

Inadequate resources

Sometimes, the only thing blocking your ideas is a lack of adequate resources. Strictly speaking, this doesn't really stop you having great ideas, but it can prevent those ideas from ever being realized. Lack of funding, technology, time, equipment, space or human resources could prevent your best ideas from ever seeing the light of day. In fairness, this tends to be more of a problem for product designers than it does for advertising creatives.

Advertising budgets may often present a challenge, but the best ideas shouldn't necessarily rely on the client spending more than they can afford. Tight deadlines may also limit the amount of ideas that you can generate within the given time-frame, but most art directors and copywriters would agree that deadlines ultimately help to focus creativity.

Right
The first helicopter
This drawing by Leonardo da Vinci (circa 1490) outlined the first design for a helicopter. However, the technology to successfully build the aircraft wasn't available at the time.

Below
Group meetings
Some group meetings and discussions don't always provide the most fertile ground for producing innovative or provocative ideas. It really depends on the attitudes and creative vision of the group members.

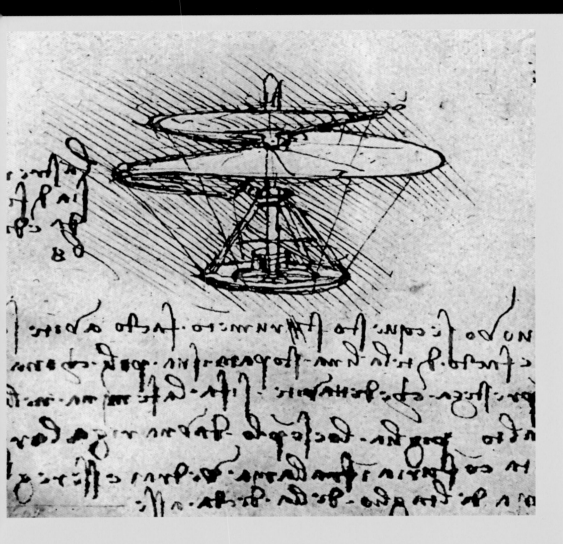

External blocks

Other people

The views and opinions of others will have an effect on how you view and judge your own ideas. None of us are completely bulletproof when it comes to negative comments regarding our ideas. However, as an advertising creative you *will* have to develop a certain resilience to negative feedback very early on. The important thing is to try to recognize the difference between helpful feedback or constructive criticism and general negativity.

As a student, when you start to show your book around to agency creatives in order to get some feedback, you can expect some hard truths about your work. If they don't tell you when they think your work is rubbish (and why) then they're not doing you any favours. The key thing at this stage is to show that you are responsive to their advice and that you can bounce back and return to the agency the following week with even better ideas. There's a big difference between this kind of feedback and the negative attitudes you may experience from other people who may have different motives for rejecting your ideas.

As an advertising creative you *will* have to develop a certain resilience to negative feedback very early on

Hopefully, you'll be surrounding yourself with friends, colleagues, team members and other people who share your vision and are generally open-minded and positive in the way that they view fresh and sometimes radically different ideas. However, you may not always be in such a fortunate position and could often find that other stakeholders in a creative project may, for a variety of different reasons, be too quick to reject your idea before you've had a fair chance to test it. You may even reject the idea yourself if you sense that it might not be very popular with those stakeholders.

Working directly with a partner (your art director or copywriter) could prove a great antidote to these situations. If you find the right kind of partner, you're not only going to be more productive; you'll also provide each other with a good sounding board for testing ideas and have more confidence to propose some of the radical ones that might prove more difficult to sell.

Adequacy

Having pre-existing solutions already in place that are adequate for their purpose can of course be a reason for abandoning any search for new ideas or solutions. After all – why bother, when what you already have still works? In all competitive domains, there is a constant need to keep ahead of the game. Leading brands spend a major part of their annual marketing budget on advertising campaigns that are constantly evolving their current themes and storylines, or re-inventing them to create new and original ones.

Brand leaders often take big risks to create new campaigns that are radically different from all that has been seen or used before in respect to that type of product category or genre. In the early 90s, Britvic used an image of a bald man, painted orange from head to foot and dressed in a loin cloth, who went about slapping people across the face in order to demonstrate the taste of their fizzy orange drink, Tango. Then, at the end of that decade, Levi's used a head-banging yellow glove puppet called Flat-Eric to revitalize the brand. In 2007, Cadbury's used a drum-playing gorilla to promote their chocolate. All of these creative strategies represented a big departure from the brands' past advertising strategies. They were all, at the time, unexpected and controversial; but each one succeeded in raising the brand's profile and keeping it ahead of the competition.

Searching for alternative solutions, even when adequate ones already exist, is typical of all truly creative thinkers

All creative strategies and solutions have a limited shelf life. They have to either evolve or change. In time, competitors will either copy, emulate or surpass them, and so it's always necessary to try to set the trend rather than to follow it. This is true in all creative domains, which is why in the field of sports, manufacturers of sports clothing and equipment are always looking at ways to improve the performance of their products, just as athletes themselves are constantly looking for ways to jump higher, run faster, throw further and generally compete at a higher level. When you think of it in this way, it's easy to see why adequacy just *isn't* good enough! Searching for alternative solutions, even when adequate ones already exist, is typical of all truly creative thinkers.

Interview ● Simon Cenamor and Raymond Chan of HMDG

Having ideas: when less isn't more

If you're an advertising creative, it's not enough to have just one or two great ideas from time to time. The most successful creative teams have the ability to generate a substantial volume of ideas at an impressive rate. In order to do this, you can't afford to judge your idea at the initial brainstorming stage. The secret is to just put it down on paper and move on to the next idea. There will be plenty of time to scrutinize each idea and assess its worth as a real solution to the brief later on.

One team that are well aware of this are copywriter, Simon Cenamor, and art director, Raymond Chan, of the British agency HMDG. After graduating from university in 2003, Simon met Raymond at theartschool; a series of free events run on an ad hoc basis at various London venues by leading creative director, Graham Fink. Theartschool provided an opportunity for young creatives to obtain advice, discuss ideas, work on briefs and find creative partners. In Simon and Raymond's case, it provided all of this and more.

How did you get started?

SC & RC:

It all started with some advice from Graham Fink, now creative director at M&C Saatchi. He suggested writing 100 ads a day. He reckons the odds are that at least one ad out of 100 would have to be pretty good. And it also means that you don't stick with your first idea. You move on, you start thinking more laterally, and you find things in places you never thought you would.

So that's what Raymond and I did. We produced stacks and stacks of ideas, and the next time we saw Graham we dumped them on his desk. It took him a few hours to get through it all, but there were a few good ads in there, and he was impressed with our effort. So impressed, that he got us a meeting with the creative director at Leith London. We didn't have a book at the time – that was what the 100-a-day ideas were working towards – so we just went in with a huge wad of ideas, and another huge wad of blank paper, which we promised to fill every week that we were on placement. He gave us a month, and we fulfilled our promise, getting in early, staying late and producing literally hundreds of ideas. After five months, and a fair amount of layout pads, we were hired.

The little goat

Simon and Raymond adopted a
Portuguese fable to demonstrate
the generous spirit of Nando's.
Copywriter: Simon Cenamor
Art Director: Raymond Chan
Agency: Farm
Director: Emma Lazenby
Production Company: Aardman

Interview ● Simon Cenamor and Raymond Chan of HMDG

Try life in another language
Produced by Simon and Raymond, this campaign targeted a hard-to-reach youth audience with the message that learning another language can be fun.
Copywriter: Simon Cenamor
Art Director: Raymond Chan
Agency: Farm
Director: Daniel Cohen, Angry Natives, Daniel Lumb, Anne Xiao
Production Company: Th1ng

What did you work on next?

SC & RC:

After several years at Leith, we moved on to work at another agency, Farm, where we produced work for several major brands. One of these brands was Nando's.

Nando's already has a huge (somewhat cult) following (they have over 350,000 fans on Facebook, for example). The brief here was to encourage trial amongst non-users by communicating everything that Nando's loyalists love about the place – the "help yourself" approach to service, the heartfelt generosity, the vibrant atmosphere and, of course, the fresh, flame-grilled Peri-Peri chicken.

What we came up with was "The Spirit of Nando's. A philosophy of Latin hospitality and great tasting chicken". The word was spread through a radio and press campaign, as well as this Portuguese fable of "The Little Goat", whose mother and father gave him as much milk as he wanted – a bit like Nando's, where you get free refills on your soft drinks. The only difference is that at Nando's, they don't put you on a spit and roast you afterwards!

Which accounts do you work on now?

SC & RC:

Another account that we recently produced work for is the UK's Department of Children, Schools and Families (DCSF).

With modern foreign languages becoming no longer compulsory as part of British school-leaving qualifications, the brief was to reverse the decline in pupils choosing to study them. The idea was to connect with this hard-to-reach audience through the things that they're already into – music, sport and other activities – only in a completely different language.

Since getting our first job in advertising, we have also worked on other major accounts, such as Hotpoint, Options, the telephone directory service Maureen 118 212, Goodfellas and National Book Tokens.

Now, a few years down the line, we don't produce that many ideas every day. But working that way has definitely taught us how to generate ideas fast, and to not be so precious about our first thoughts. It also makes a blank piece of paper look a lot less scary.

Twenty ideas in twenty minutes

Now that you know why it's so important to have lots of different ideas every time you get a brief, you'll need to train yourself to have ideas quickly without spending too much time judging them at the outset – you can always assess them later. For the moment, it's about quantity, not quality, so here's an exercise that will help you to develop your creative fluency.

In order to prepare for this, you'll need a friend, colleague or tutor to write out a list of imaginary products along with details of their key benefit or selling proposition. The list might look something like this: garlic that's odourless; electrically heated gloves for the winter; golf balls that send out a GPS signal so that you can locate them; a restaurant for dogs... and so on. Around 12 of these will do. They can be unusual, crazy, interesting or provide just a slight twist on something that already exists. You'll need a cheap layout pad, a medium-size black marker pen and some means of timing yourself, such as a stopwatch.

Randomly select one of the products from the list. You can do this by having each of the 12 products written on individual bits of paper that you can draw from a container, lottery style.

Now set the stopwatch and give yourself one minute to sketch out an idea on the layout pad. At the end of that minute, start on a new page and have another idea in one minute. Once again, after a minute, start on a fresh sheet of paper and have a fresh idea and so on for 20 minutes. At the end of that time, you should have 20 ideas.

Quick draw!

Here's a fun class (or group) exercise that will also help you to increase your creative output. It's based on the preceding exercise but this time you can play it as a two-person competition where you pit your wits against another member of the class or group. The two of you, each armed with just a black marker pen and a flip chart, each have only 30 seconds to sketch out an idea in response to a given product. As with the previous exercise, it should be a product with a key benefit or selling proposition which should be given to both you and your challenger at the same time.

After 30 seconds, both of you have to stop drawing and it's up to the class or group to vote for a winner by deciding which idea they like best. The winner stays on and is then challenged to a quick draw by another member of the class. This time, a new product is given to you by the class and once again the two competing members of the class have 30 seconds to quickly sketch out their first idea. Once again, the class vote for the winner who then stays on. You should continue this exercise until everyone has had a chance to compete – and longer if you're still having fun.

Summing up

Both of these exercises will deny you the time to think too hard or for too long. You just have to run with the first idea or image that comes into your head. In doing so, you will come to learn that you can have lots of ideas quickly if you don't judge them as you're having them. Whilst many of the ideas will be unworkable, some of them are likely to provide you with a springboard to a fresh way of seeing the advertising problem, or an alternative idea.

Certain things can block ideas or prevent you from having fresh ones. Even the most accomplished advertising creatives sometimes have a bad day when the creative juices just don't seem to be flowing. At those times, it feels like the harder you try to find a creative solution, the more elusive it becomes.

Later on in the book, we'll be looking at specific tools, techniques and approaches you can use to stimulate ideas, but let's begin by looking at some general things that you can do to kick-start creativity. These include breaking routine, experimentation, re-interpreting the problem, interrogating the brief, learning to think laterally, challenging assumptions, cultivating your powers of observation, developing your curiosity and having the courage to take risks.

Breaking routine

There's little doubt that routine can kill creativity. The more that we get used to doing or seeing things in a certain way, the less likely we are to try new ways of tackling or viewing those things. Routine provides us with a guaranteed means of getting the job done – for everyday tasks in the workplace and in our daily lives, ritualized behaviour informs and governs both what we do and how we do it. However, the longer we pursue routine, the more difficult it becomes to abandon it in favour of a fresh approach or perspective.

Experimentation allows you to discover things that you hadn't seen or known before

Changing habits

One way to start breaking routine is to begin by changing some of our habits. Habitual behaviour has an effect on everything we do. It establishes routine patterns of working that before long become ingrained as formulated approaches to tasks or problems. The reason we can so readily slip into a routine approach is that it provides us with a tried-and-tested template for tackling those tasks or problems that we are faced with on a regular basis.

If a particular way of doing things has become part of our routine, then we can be almost certain of the outcome. It's that certainty that provides us with a sense of

Doing things differently to see things differently

Routine enables us to achieve certain goals or objectives with very little thought or extra effort. It often enables us to get from A to B by the shortest and most certain route. This is fine when there's no need for creativity or alternative solutions. However, when we start to adopt routine approaches for tackling projects that could benefit from some fresh thinking or new solutions, then we are unlikely to see all of the opportunities that are presented to us.

Changing even just one daily habit can have a ripple effect on how we view or approach the rest of our tasks that day. Something as simple as travelling into work by a different route one morning can break the routine patterns of thinking that are established at the beginning of the day and stay with us throughout it. Once those patterns are broken, it can become easier to explore new ways of doing things, which in turn can stimulate a fresh outlook on everything that we are subsequently confronted with.

One senior creative team working at a London advertising agency used to swap seats every time that they found themselves stuck for an idea. They found that this simple change in routine would often be enough to give them a fresh perspective on the problem and to stimulate further ideas.

Experimenting

Things start happening when we break with routine and stop to take a fresh look at the problems or tasks that confront us. We can start to explore alternative ways of doing and seeing things. When you're looking for new ideas for an advertising campaign, the creative brief will get you started, but the next stage is to experience the product for yourself and to find a new way of expressing that experience and the product benefit through your ideas.

Experiment with the product, see what happens if you take it apart, turn it upside down, inside out or even combine it with something else. Look at it from different viewpoints and angles – could it look like something else? How else could it be used, or even misused? The brief may give you some insights on what to do here.

For example, if the proposition states that the product is tough and hard-wearing, then you might think about testing it to destruction in extreme conditions. If the proposition states that the product is 'reliable', then experiment with the product to find a novel way to demonstrate this reliability, either literally or metaphorically. Essentially, try to find another way of showing the product or service that demonstrates the proposition or benefit in a visually surprising and unusual way. Experimentation allows you to discover things that you hadn't seen or didn't know before. You can then pass this discovery onto your audience to make the advertising at once both more engaging and memorable.

Breaking routine

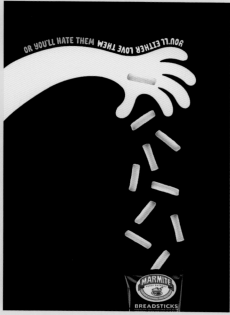

Love them or hate them?

This campaign for Marmite Snacks took the brand insight ('You either love it or hate it') a stage further. By experimenting with different illustrative visuals and the way in which shapes can be interpreted in a range of ways when inverted or rotated, the creative team came up with this clever way of demonstrating the paradoxical nature of the snacks – that you'll either love them or hate them!

Agency: DDB UK
Illustrator: Al Murphy

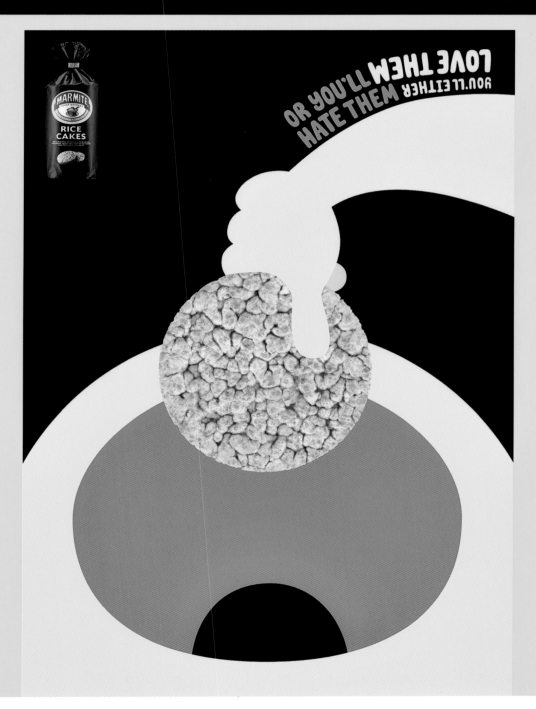

Re-interpreting the problem

One sure way to find new solutions is to first find new ways of seeing the problem itself. In Chapter 1, we looked at how mind sets can channel thinking in a certain direction. When we first get the creative brief, we tend to refer back to similar briefs or products and past advertising solutions, sometimes making it difficult to escape from creating a campaign for your client's new product that essentially looks like every other campaign that's been produced by similar or competing products. One way to prevent this from happening is to look at ways of re-interpreting the brief. This doesn't mean changing it, but refers to simply changing the way in which you view it.

Interrogating the brief

The starting point for great ideas is the creative brief. In different agencies, the creative brief is written in a variety of diverse ways and comes in all sorts of sizes, styles and formats. Its design often tends to reflect the creative ethos of the agency. In some cases, there will be an excess of information and perhaps even some suggestions on alternative routes that could be explored or other brand insights that may be worth pursuing. In other cases, the brief may be very minimal and contain only one or two paragraphs of information, leaving you to make your own discoveries.

Most briefs will contain the same kind of information, which will include the key things you'll need to know about the campaign; what you're selling, who you're selling it to, why they would want to buy it (the advertising proposition), the advertising objectives and the choice of media.

One way to get the most out of the brief is to start questioning each point in turn. For example, if the brief is to create a poster campaign for the new Toyota open-top saloon car aimed at young professional men, then ask yourself why young professionals would want the car. How would they feel driving one? How might it change their lives? Is it a car you're selling, or really something else – such as status, dreams, or sex on four wheels? The brief will only tell you so much. It's up to you to use a combination of interrogation and imagination to work out what the brief *isn't* telling you. Asking questions is the key to creativity, and the real skill is in identifying what questions you should be asking.

❝

Asking questions is the key to creativity, and the real skill is in identifying what questions you should be asking

❞

Getting to the heart of the real problem

Somewhere between the advertising proposition and the advertising objectives, the creative brief should give you a sense of what the real problem for the brand is – its reason for advertising. It could be, for instance, that the brand has a poor reputation for service or performance, or that it's not very visible and needs to raise awareness, or that it now comes with extra benefits. However the brief defines the problem, it's your job to dig deeper. For example, if the campaign has to help improve the reputation of the brand then you first have to look at why the brand has a poor reputation in the first place. Is it deserved and what have the brand owners done to improve performance or service since? If the problem is lack of awareness or invisibility in a competitive market, you have to once again ask why this is. In these situations, you may be looking for ways to turn a negative aspect into a positive one.

What do the audience really want?

Getting to the root of what your target audience really want is a fundamental part of the process. It involves putting yourself in their place and empathizing with them. If you're advertising something that is going to benefit your audience in some way, ask yourself whether they really *do* need this product and what kind of difference it will actually make to their lives. What might their lives currently be like without those benefits?

Of course, you do have to be careful that you're not trying to demonstrate that your client's new brand of bottle opener is going to change the world. However, in this case, you could perhaps use comic scenarios (illustrating, for instance, the kind of things people do to open their bottle of beer when they don't have a bottle opener), to demonstrate what a difference your client's product could make, injecting some fun into the campaign at the same time.

You need to convince the target audience that you understand them and the problems that they may face. One way you can do this is by basing your idea on an experience that they can immediately relate to. You need the audience to be nodding in agreement with what you have to say. Get them thinking: 'That's so true!'

Re-interpreting the problem

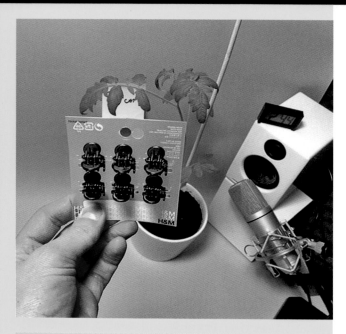

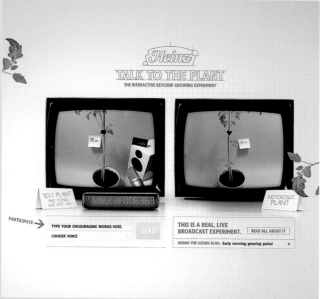

Left
Talk to the plant
In order to substantiate their new tagline 'No one grows ketchup like Heinz', their advertising agency chose to not just say it, but to also demonstrate it in an unusual and interactive way. On the associated website, visitors were invited to talk to a tomato plant via voice synthesis in real time and watch to see if it resulted in greater growth than the reference plant. Everything spoken to the plant was broadcast live on the site and a blog logged each message and recorded plant growth.
Client: Heinz

Right
Barcode
Faux barcodes concealed a coded helpline number for women who were victims of domestic violence. They could be discreetly stuck on any domestic object to remain unnoticed by the perpetrators of the violence.
Agency: TBWA New Zealand
Photographer: Andy Blood

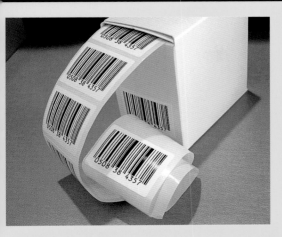

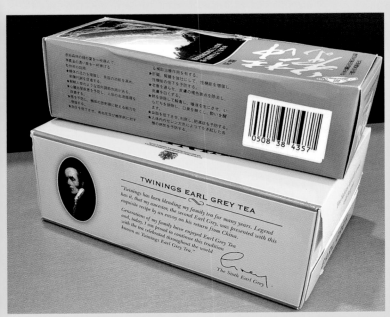

Lateral thinking

'Lateral thinking' was a term coined by Edward de Bono in the 60s, to describe a way of thinking that enables us to find alternative solutions and ideas that would not normally be accessed through conventional, rational or routine ways of approaching problems. It normally involves techniques and approaches that use unconventional methods for disrupting logical or linear thinking by breaking mindsets and creating 'provocations'. These provocations enable the problem solver to make a lateral jump to alternative ideas that can offer novel solutions.
We'll be looking at some of these techniques and approaches in the next chapter, but first let's take a look at some of the basic principles that will help you to have great advertising ideas.

Searching for alternatives

We've already learnt about the need for divergent thinking as a way to find alternative ideas and solutions, and recognized that this process is the essence of creativity. Lateral thinking can provide a systematic means of prompting alternative ideas and for this reason it's a particularly useful tool for advertising creatives. When you're working on a brief, it's your ability to find alternative ideas to those previously used by the brand and its competitors that define your creative fluency. It's also possible to have a good idea that blocks you from having more good ideas. When you do have an idea that you're really pleased with, it's difficult to put that aside and have another good idea, and then another, and so on. Always be aware that there may be a better idea just around the corner, and that there's always an alternative solution to a creative brief.

Edward de Bono uses the analogy of 'digging for buried treasure' to illustrate the use of lateral thinking in discovering alternative solutions. He explains that you can keep digging deeper but never discover the treasure that's buried just below the surface and just to the side of the hole that you're digging. You have to be prepared to leave the hole you're digging to start afresh elsewhere. The longer and deeper you dig away at the same hole, the more difficult this lateral shift becomes. Similarly, the longer you pursue the same direction searching for an idea, the more difficult it becomes to look in other directions.

Zigging while the others are zagging

John Hegarty, founding partner and worldwide creative director of the advertising agency BBH, once said 'when the world zigs, zag'; suggesting that we should be doing the opposite to what everyone else is doing. There's little doubt that the success of a brand leader is determined by its capacity to originate rather than imitate. This is expressed through the products and services they offer, the way in which they conduct their business, their corporate ethos and their marketing communication, in which advertising will normally play a vital role.

When it comes to creating advertising campaigns that are different from everyone else's, there are two things to remember. First, it's important not to be different just for the sake of it. Make sure that the radically different ideas that you settle on are different in a way that's relevant to (or that directly reflects) some aspect of the brand itself. Secondly, remember that fresh ideas will eventually go stale, and that you should constantly be looking in new directions for inspiration and a change to the way in which you communicate the advertising message. Innovative ideas tend to be copied and they soon become trends. In order to keep one step ahead of the competition, you need to be ready to change direction at the right time.

There's little doubt that the success of a brand leader is determined by its capacity to originate, rather than to imitate

The secret of lateral thinking

Generally speaking, lateral thinking involves a two-stage process. The first stage involves identifying all of the possible assumptions you could be making with regard to the problem itself and the content within the creative brief. The second stage involves challenging each of those assumptions in turn, to see what ideas and opportunities open up. This all sounds very easy when described like this; however, the most difficult part is identifying all of the assumptions that we could be making in the first place. Many of these assumptions will arise from deep-seated mindsets that we may already have, and these can be very hard to escape from. In the next section, we'll take a look at the kind of assumptions we might be making when we get a creative brief.

Lateral thinking

Lateral thinking

These adverts for Coroa hand tools
demonstrate the usefulness of the
product with a lateral thought that
expresses the strapline 'It's a quick fix'
in a witty, alternative fashion.
Client: Coroa hand tools
Product: Sledgehammer
Creative Directors:
Anselmo Ramos, Denis Kakuzu
Art Directors: Denis Kakuzu,
Paulo Engler, Adriana Franco
Copywriters:
Rafael Campos, Erick Stossel

Challenging assumptions

The creative brief will specify what you're selling, who you're selling it to and what media you can use to advertise it. However, it's easy for even the most creative person to start making assumptions about each of these areas almost immediately. As with any other creative problem, by challenging these assumptions head on, we can endeavour to find new lateral solutions.

What are we assuming about the audience?

A good creative brief will use more than just socio-economic groupings to construct a profile of the target audience. It could cover everything from their lifestyles, hobbies, interests, qualifications and employment, through to their beliefs, opinions, or tastes in food, drink, music and entertainment. The sum of all of this should provide you with a fairly clear image of that person. However, even with a clear image of who we're talking to, we might still make assumptions about that person or stereotype them.

One way round this is to identify all the things that you could be assuming about the target audience. Why would they want the product that you're advertising? If it's a shampoo brand for women, the brief may tell you that 'it gives you hair that is soft and shiny', so it's fair to assume that your target audience want soft, shiny hair. But as soon as you challenge this assumption and state that 'the target audience don't want soft and shiny hair', you can prompt yourself to ask 'what are their real reasons for wanting the product?' It could be that they want to get noticed, or to feel good about themselves, or simply that they liked the attention they attracted last time they used the shampoo. This gives you more scope for fresh ideas. Rather than just talking about how your hair feels so soft after using the shampoo (like most other shampoo ads do), you can instead show what happens when you feel good about yourself, or how you feel when a stranger comments on how great your hair looks.

Don't lose your contacts when you drop your phone
Airtel offer a data backup service for mobile phones. In this campaign, they address the problems people face when they lose their mobile phone. It's easy to assume that the greatest concern is for the lost phone itself, but it's more likely the consequences of losing the data on your phone, with all your contacts' details, that is more worrying.
Agency: REDIFFUSION Y&R Gurgaon
Client: Bharti Airtel
Executive Creative Directors:
Jaideep Mahajan, Deepesh Jha
Photographer: Tarun Vishwa

Challenging assumptions

What are we assuming about the product?

Consider what you could be assuming about the product. If it's a camera, it's easy to assume that your target audience may want it to capture images – but what happens if we challenge this assumption? What do they really want a camera for? Perhaps they want it to capture memories, or to record an important event. Maybe they just want to look good by being seen to own it, or perhaps they want to give it to someone else as a gift.

It can be quite difficult to leave all the past images of what camera adverts generally look like behind you in order to tackle the brief with a completely fresh mind. One good place to start is to do something totally unexpected. For example, if it's an advert for power tools that you're working on, take a look at all of the power tool campaigns that you can find. You'll probably discover that most of them have the same kind of style and approach in the way that they're executed. Consider using a style of advertising that is totally different from all the other power tool adverts that you've seen, in terms of style or content. How about creating it in the style of a health campaign or a commercial for a telephone directory, for instance? Of course, you may find yourself heading off in completely the wrong direction, but it's a direction that's worth exploring!

> **You may find yourself heading off in completely the wrong direction, but it's a direction that's worth exploring!**

What are we assuming about the media?

It's relatively easy to make assumptions about advertising media as we're so used to seeing traditional media being used in conventional ways. Yet as soon as we see something we're familiar with presented in an *unfamiliar* way, it instantly grabs our attention. So it's worth looking at new ways of using old media, alongside the fresh approaches that new media already provides.

Ask yourself: 'What can I do that's different in the way that I use or present the media?' For example, can you use traditional print media in a way that engages the other senses – not just sight? Can you use media that's normally used for still images to instead portray moving images? Can you position the media in an unconventional way? We tend to assume that press and poster adverts will be squared-up, highly visible and easy to read. What happens if we challenge these assumptions and do something different? Where does that lead us?

We make assumptions that we'll normally find poster sites by the roadside or in places where there's a high volume of people around. How about challenging this assumption to place posters in locations where there are very few people? This may sound a little crazy at first, but think of it as a springboard idea and see where it takes you. It may lead you to the idea of placing the poster in a place where only your target audience are likely to be found. Imagine the impact of a poster advertising scuba equipment if that poster is placed underwater at a tropical dive site frequented by scuba divers and underwater enthusiasts.

It's relatively easy to make assumptions about advertising media as we're so used to seeing traditional media being used in conventional ways. Yet as soon as we see something we're familiar with presented in an *unfamiliar* way, it instantly grabs our attention

Think about all of the other assumptions that you could be making about the advertising media. Not just where it's placed, but how it's placed and when it's placed. Can it perhaps change shape or colour, deteriorate or decay over time? Could it be given some kind of tactile quality or emit a sound or smell? Does it have to be static or can it move around? The range of different assumptions that you could challenge is limitless and can lead you to media-based ideas that grab attention and create impact. However, at the end of the day you should of course check that the manner in which you choose to do this has some relevance to the advertising message and that it helps to communicate the brand proposition in some way.

Challenging assumptions

Magic salad plate

Instead of hiding the fact that their brand isn't the healthiest choice of food, Four 'n Twenty Meat Pies embrace this in an integrated campaign which features images of salad printed on paper plates – so that you can fool people into thinking you're eating a healthy meal.

Agency: Clemenger BBDO Melbourne, Australia

Account Directors:
Sarah Galbraith, Ricci Meldrum
Creative team:
Julian Schreiber, Tom Martin
Creative Director: Ant Keogh
Director: Tony Rogers/DOP
Cinematographer: Marin Johnson
Images: all rights and images remain the property of Clemenger BBDO Melbourne and cannot be reproduced without written permission.

Observation, curiosity and experience

The ability to see things differently and to notice the details that other people take for granted is a characteristic of the best creative thinkers. When linked with a questioning approach to problem solving, it becomes a key creative skill that's at the root of lateral thinking. By also drawing from our own unique experiences in how we view and approach creative problems, we can create solutions that are equally unique.

Right
Test
Casa do Zezinho is an educational 'safehouse' for impoverished children living on the outskirts of São Paolo in Brazil. This commercial for the organization presents us with a closer look at an aspect of human nature. It features a test where the split-screen format shows the same child actor walking the streets of São Paolo dressed in expensive clothes and in clothes that make him look like a child from the streets. The footage showed that people only stopped to ask if he was alright when he was dressed in the more expensive clothes.
© Casa do Zezinho/AlmapBBDO/ Cinema Centro

Looking closer at the product

When you're trying to find a new way to express the advertising message, or a different way to show the product, it's important to look beyond the common visual image of the product as most people know it. When you have the product in front of you and you really study it for a while, you'll notice things about it that you haven't seen before. From a certain angle or viewpoint, it might look like something else. By removing a part, or dismantling it, you could highlight another aspect of the product, such as the craftsmanship, precision or the amount of work and detail that goes into its manufacturing. Then you can start experimenting further. with the product, as described earlier in this chapter. The opportunities to 'play' with the product and discover something new about it are endless.

Try focusing in on detail. When asked to think about what a pair of shoes look like, we visualize them as a whole – not as a close-up of the stitching in the leather or the lacing. By focusing in on detail we can create a more interesting, unusual, unexpected and visually compelling image – one that can express an aspect of the proposition in a more dramatic or intriguing way. Of course, it's not always a product that you may be examining – it could be something less tangible, such as a service or an issue. It could be the target audience themselves or even human nature that you're putting under the magnifying glass in your ad.

Matheus Braga, 5 anos   Matheus Braga, 5 anos

Por que algumas crianças
são problema nosso
e outras não?

Observation, curiosity and experience

Discover something interesting about the product

Of course, looking closer isn't just about finding unusual ways to show the product. It's also about getting to the heart of the problem and really understanding consumer needs. Whether it's a product, service or special cause that you're writing an advert for, your ideas may be the latest in a long-running campaign where the advertising proposition remains the same; that it's faster, cheaper, bigger, smaller, safer, better quality, fruitier, tastier, or something else along these lines. Your challenge is to find a different way to say the same thing each time, otherwise your audience will lose interest. Big brands build their reputations on having clear and consistent brand messages; but finding a new way to demonstrate the same brand message every time you write an advert for that brand is the real test of creativity.

However you choose to show the product in your campaign, the most important thing is to grab attention and then hold your audience's interest. One way to do this is to find out something novel about the product, or an interesting fact that can be related to the product, and to play it back to the audience through your advertising. Here's an interesting fact: 'one of the most dangerous insects in the world is the common housefly, as they carry and transmit more diseases than any other animal in the world'. Now, if you're advertising a brand of fly spray, that could (with suitable crafting) provide an attention-grabbing headline capable of compelling the reader to read on into the body copy.

In order to sound interesting, you need to tell your audience something they don't already know, and the chances are if you know it already, then so do they. That's why it's important to set out to discover fresh facts, stories and anecdotes about the product. Even the most trivial facts can grab attention and engage your audience. Asking lots of questions about every aspect of the product from its conception and production, through to its final usage, can reveal interesting facts and snippets that you may be able to use somewhere in the campaign, so above all, remain curious.

Right
Grabbing attention with copy
These copy-led ads describe in graphic detail what happens to human eyes after death, offering a persuasive argument in favour of eye donation.
Agency: Creativeland Asia, Mumbai
Client: Eye Bank Association, Kerala
Copywriter:
Sajan Raj Kurup, Anu Joseph
Art Director: Vikram Gaikwad
Creative Directors: Sajan Raj Kurup, Anu Joseph, Vikram Gaikwad

IF YOU ARE A PARSEE,

ABOUT THIRTY VULTURES ARRIVE AT YOUR DEAD BODY EVEN AS THE LAST MAN FROM YOUR FUNERAL PROCESSION WALKS OUT OF THE TOWER OF SILENCE. VULTURES ARE INSTINCTIVELY FAMILIAR TO THE NATURE OF THE HUMAN BODY. THEY KNOW THAT YOUR EYES ARE THE MOST DELICATE PART OF YOU. IN AN INSTANT, THE BIRDS GATHER BY YOUR HEAD. RAVENOUSLY HUNGRY AND FIERCELY COMPETITIVE, THEY DON'T PECK AT YOUR EYES. THEY DIG INTO THEM. YOUR EYELIDS ARE TORN APART IN A MOMENT. AND YOUR EYEBALLS ARE PUNCTURED. THE AQUEOUS AND VITREOUS HUMOURS LEAK OUT. QUICKLY, BIT BY BIT, YOUR EYEBALLS ARE PICKED OUT OF THEIR SOCKETS. THE OPTIC NERVE AND ALL THE OTHER HUNDREDS OF BLOOD VESSELS ARE RIPPED OUT ALONG WITH THEM. YOUR CORNEA AND RETINA, OF COURSE, STAND NO CHANCE AS THE FEAST BEGINS.

NO I DON'T WANT TO PLEDGE MY EYES TO THE VULTURES. PLEASE GET IN TOUCH WITH ME.

MY NAME:_____

ADDRESS:_____

PHONE NO.:_____ E-MAIL ID:_____

PLEASE MAIL THIS COUPON TO:
EYE BANK ASSOCIATION KERALA, CBM OPTHALMIC INSTITUTE, LITTLE FLOWER HOSPITAL & RESEARCH CENTRE, ANGAMALY-683 573, KERALA.

IF YOU ARE A CHRISTIAN,

THE ORNATE WOODEN COFFIN FIRST DELAYS THE DECOMPOSITION PROCESS OF YOUR DEAD BODY, AND THEN HURRIES IT UP. BACTERIA BEGIN TO FORM AT ALL RELATIVELY SOFTER SPOTS IN YOUR BODY. YOUR EYES, WET AND DELICATE THAT THEY ARE, USUALLY ARE THE FIRST TARGETS. SOON, A STICKY CORNEAL FILM FORMS OVER YOUR EYES. AND UGLY BLACK SPOTS APPEAR ON THE WHITE TISSUE. INDIVIDUAL CELLS IN YOUR EYES BEGIN TO DIE, RELEASING ENZYMES THAT BREAK DOWN THE CELL MATERIAL AND CONNECTIONS TO OTHER CELLS. GASES ARE CONTINUOUSLY RELEASED AND MAKE YOUR EYES BULGE OUT AND FINALLY BURST OPEN. FLUIDS CONTINUE TO OOZE TILL YOUR EYES START SHRINKING, AND EVENTUALLY DECOMPOSE INTO A GOOEY MASS. IF THE SOIL AROUND YOUR COFFIN IS LOOSE AND HAS WORMS AND OTHER CREEPY CREATURES IN IT, THEN THE STORY GETS GORIER.

NO I DON'T WANT TO PLEDGE MY EYES TO BACTERIA AND WORMS. PLEASE GET IN TOUCH WITH ME.

MY NAME:_____

ADDRESS:_____

PHONE NO.:_____ E-MAIL ID:_____

PLEASE MAIL THIS COUPON TO:
EYE BANK ASSOCIATION KERALA, CBM OPTHALMIC INSTITUTE, LITTLE FLOWER HOSPITAL & RESEARCH CENTRE, ANGAMALY-683 573, KERALA.

Observation, curiosity and experience

Tap into your experience

The best way to really understand the product and what it's offering the consumer, is to experience or sample it for yourself. Try using it for a while and you may find some hidden benefits that are worth talking about in your campaign, or a novel way of demonstrating the central proposition. If you're writing an advert for a new ride at an amusement park, actually trying the ride out for yourself, together with the entire range of physical sensations – from exhilaration to nausea – you'll be likely to experience, will give you the insights that your imagination alone cannot access. If it's something you're unable to experience personally, then talk to people who already have. What have they got to say about it?

In addition to the specific brand experience, there are your own, more general life experiences that you can tap into for ideas. Each of us has our own personal way of seeing and interpreting the world about us, based on our past and present experiences. However, there are some human experiences and behavioural patterns that generally tend to be shared across society.

Dinner

This advert for a law firm humorously shows how our most commonplace deeds could become subject to legal action; and how the simple act of cooking dinner could be potentially litigious if the instructions are not carefully followed, thereby exempting the 'chef' from any legal responsibility. It taps into readers' knowledge of such disclaimers at the point where legal necessity meets absurdity.
Agency: M & C Saatchi
Creative Director and Copywriter: Ben Welsh
Art Director and Photographer: Chris Round
Client:
Lyndon Sayer-Jones and Associates

In the 90s, British copywriter David Abbott wrote a TV commercial for British Telecom featuring a young girl phoning home from university. In the scene, her father picks up the phone at the other end, and the first thing he says when he realizes it's his daughter, is: '…I'll go and get your mother.' Abbott realized that hundreds of fathers across the country (including himself) were doing this, and that by re-playing it in a commercial, the advertising was more likely to make a connection and prompt them to reflect on the advertising message: 'It's good to talk.' Simple observations of human nature can provide excellent material for advertising creatives. For this reason, it's important to capture and record them in some way; you never know when they're going to be useful.

Your dinner is in the oven.
Cook for 30minutes at 240c or 45secs in the microwave under 'reheat' setting.
Failure to follow these instructions may result in the consumer of this meal suffering E. coli food poisoning for which, I the undersigned, accept no responsibility whatsoever.
Nor is any responsibility accepted for any oral burns resulting from consuming this meal immediately after removing it from the oven or microwave.
Love Jenny
xxx
www.lsj.com.au
Lyndon Sayer-Jones & Associates
Lawyers

Risk-taking

There's plenty of advertising, but not much of it is original. When a brand risks trying something different from the advertising typical to a type of product, there's a good chance the campaign could fail or worse still, damage the brand itself. Yet, to stay at the top, brand leaders have to take risks as success is often determined by a capacity to originate and innovate. This is apparent in everything they do, say or produce – not least, their advertising.

Why originality requires risk

Leading advertising creative Graham Fink once said: 'If you know what you're doing, you can't be doing anything original.' The implication here is that if you know what you're doing, it's because it's been done before, and if that's the case, it can't be original. To have an original idea, you have to be prepared to explore directions and routes that you've never tried out before. This means temporarily suspending logic and freeing yourself up to have some of those wild and crazy ideas that we mentioned earlier. Be aware though that this way of working is a bit more hit and miss, and that not all of your ideas will provide original solutions that meet the advertising objectives.

Risks are taken at various stages of the process. You'll be taking risks when you share your initial springboard ideas with friends, colleagues or members of your team. Hopefully, a mixture of trust, together with the licence to have wild ideas at the early stage of the process, will lessen this risk. The presentation of final ideas to the creative director of the agency and then the client are the next levels of risk, and in the latter case could have serious implications for the agency and the creative team if they get it wrong. Finally, there's the risk the client or brand takes if the idea is accepted and launched. Although research can reduce the risk, no one really knows at this stage whether the chosen campaign will be successful or not, and the more original it is, the greater the risk that's taken.

Whilst logical thinking can be abandoned during the initial phases of divergent thinking, at some stage all of those wild ideas need to be harvested and rationalized alongside the criteria within the creative brief, in order to evaluate their worth and filter the ideas that are both original and relevant. This is where you can, to a certain extent, manage the risk and still present the client with a groundbreaking creative campaign. It's then up to the client to decide if they've the courage to run with it!

As a student, you may think that all of these risks are something that you won't really have to worry about until you've actually got a job. However, deciding what to include in your book (and what to exclude) each time you visit an agency with a view to getting a placement, also involves taking some risks.

Failure as a portal to success

In most circumstances, we tend to regard failure as a bad thing; however, it is inextricably linked to the creative process. Having lots of ideas inevitably means that a good proportion of them will fail to provide adequate solutions. You have to accept that not all of the routes you'll be exploring will be fruitful and that only a few of them may break through to a really creative idea that's worth pursuing. Unfortunately, there's no way of knowing at the outset which routes will be the most productive and so sometimes intuition is your best guide. This is why there's hardly ever any way of bypassing the dead end routes or pathways leading to weaker ideas. They are all part of the process that leads to the discovery of a creative solution.

Contrary to popular belief, it's rarely the case that your first idea is your best idea. It's more likely to be the most obvious idea. It's only once your initial ideas are exhausted and you have to look elsewhere for alternative solutions that the really lateral ideas start to surface. For every hundred ideas you may have, only one or two may provide you with a really original solution that fits the brief. However, failure to find the solution that you're searching for in the early stages of ideation is inevitable. The more ideas you have, the closer you'll get to a really creative idea that ticks all of the boxes.

The most fertile creative environments and cultures give individuals the freedom and space to explore different routes, make mistakes and even fail from time to time on the basis that when we explore new avenues, we have no way of knowing where they will lead, and so some level of failure is inevitable. Tolerance of failure is founded on the understanding that it's through exploration and reflection on failure that we finally break through to innovative ideas and solutions.

Serendipity and accidental creativity

It's important to recognize that many significant discoveries have emerged by chance or error. In some cases, a chance event or occurrence will prompt a creative idea nesting in our subconscious, particularly if we've already been primed with information and the advertising brief is somewhere in the back of our mind. Accidents, errors and serendipity can play a major role in the creative process as they introduce a random element that breaks routine or logical approaches to tackling the creative brief. They enable us to make alternative and sometimes analogical connections with the problem at hand. However, when the pressure is on to have a range of new ideas for an advertising campaign and the deadline is tomorrow, sometimes chance needs to be prompted. This is where some of the techniques outlined in the next chapter can help you out.

Risk-taking

Specsavers

This TV commercial for Specsavers, a UK-based chain of opticians, depicted an elderly sheep farmer hand-shearing his sheep and then proceeding to unwittingly shear his trusted sheepdog as well! The slogan 'Should have gone to Specsavers' at the end of the ad provides the comic moment by explaining the sheep farmer's erratic behaviour. It also demonstrates a strong campaignable theme, which focuses on the consequences of not buying your glasses from Specsavers.

Interview ● Nigel Clifton of EHS 4D

The evolution of ideas

Today, advertising has to work harder than ever to cut through all the competing advertising messages in a salient, memorable and compelling manner that's both relevant to the target audience and which fulfils the client's needs. Amongst other things, this involves the capacity to see things with fresh eyes, to re-interpret problems, challenge assumptions, interrogate the brief, keep asking questions, to do things differently and also to take a few risks along the way! Different advertising agencies adopt their own unique strategies and approaches to facilitate this. Creative director Nigel Clifton describes how the creative process works at his London agency, EHS 4D, over the following pages.

What is the creative process at EHS 4D?

NC:

To deliver strong creative solutions that solve problems, we adhere to a simple process that connects everyone in the agency, unlocks insights, creates ideas and delivers work to an exceptional standard. This process is made up of five stages: *Discover*, *Imagine*, *Create*, *Craft* and *Learn*. Each stage has clear outputs that help create great communications. Within the agency, we have designed rooms to reflect the key stages that lead to the generation of ideas and final concepts. *Discover* is a space designed as a school room, Imagine is a relaxing space and *Create* is a flexible space that can be used as we see fit for each campaign.

How do you get projects started?

NC:

Every project starts with *Discover*. Collectively, we get under the skin of the target audience, the brand, the category and the business to work out the best approach. In doing this, we will also clearly define the problem or opportunity.

We find out some key things... exactly who should we be aiming our campaign at? What are they like? What is important to them? What are their needs and motivation? How do they use different media? How and where do they interact with the brand? And more – we will also explore how competitors behave and communicate. This helps us to understand the opportunities to do things differently, to get cut-through, and to understand the client's business and brand, their challenges and opportunities, together with their needs and the requirements for the work. Before moving on, we have a clear set of insights that help us to understand how best to approach the brief.

How do you develop your initial ideas?

NC:

The next stage we call *Imagine*. This begins with a brainstorm, to generate possibilities and alternative approaches to the problem. We have to avoid jumping to one solution so that at the end we have a variety of ideas. Once the ideas are compiled, we review the thinking both logically and critically. This identifies the strongest solution and opportunities to the problem. From here, a clear, single-minded creative brief is written.

Next comes the *Create* stage. To get this moving, we are given a clear understanding of the task through an inspiring and comprehensive creative briefing session. This can be in the agency or in a location that is relevant to the brief. For example, if we are selling a car, then sitting in the environment that the car will be sold in will help us to bring the brief alive. All aspects of *Discover* and *Imagine* are used to inform and support the creative brief.

We then explore a number of routes that best answer the brief. Regular meetings with the creative director and team help to shape the work and make sure that the ideas reflect the brand's characteristics, the customer needs and the problem the brief intends to solve. We push the thinking within the boundaries of the brief, creating original, insightful and relevant concepts that fulfil the brief. The concepts are then presented to the client and a single concept is chosen for development.

Interview ● Nigel Clifton of EHS 4D

Discover, Imagine and Create
At the UK advertising agency EHS 4D, specially themed rooms have been designated as creative spaces for each of the initial phases of the creative process: *Discover* (right), *Imagine* (below), and *Create* (facing).

How do you produce the advertising?

NC:

The penultimate stage of the process involves the production and crafting of the advertising. In the *Craft* stage, photographers, typographers, illustrators and designers are just some of the specialists we use to enhance the concept. The art director will brief them, and the writer will execute the copy. The end result is brilliantly crafted communication that answers the brief, and visually and tonally resonates with the target audience – brilliant work we are all proud of.

How do you monitor the success of a campaign?

NC:

Once the campaign or concept is running we watch how effective it is, and from that we enter the final stage: *Learn*. Here we collate and learn from all results gained from the communication, and apply them to future projects, making the work continually better and better. We then sit down and begin the process again with *Discover*.

Give it a go ● The assumption challenge – challenge!

Challenging your own assumptions

We've seen how the key to lateral thinking involves first identifying assumptions, and then challenging them. Treat this exercise as a personal challenge. First, choose a product or brand – something you'd like to create a great campaign for. On a piece of paper, list 20 assumptions that most people would make about that product or brand. For example, does it normally come in certain colours, shapes or sizes? Is it normally dirt cheap or really expensive? Has it got a reputation for reliability or unreliability? Is it fashionable or outdated?… And so on.

You'll probably find the first few assumptions relatively easy to identify and then when you've listed the most obvious ones on your piece of paper, start to struggle to meet your quota of 20. That's all part of the challenge. Set yourself a time limit, say 20 minutes. If you're still struggling to identify 20 assumptions about the product after half an hour, then it's time to stop and move on to the next part of the exercise.

Next, produce a similar list on another piece of paper. This time, identify assumptions that people would make about the kind of people that would use or buy the product. The same rules apply: 20 assumptions in 20 minutes. These assumptions could include those we might make about gender, likes, dislikes, attitudes, opinions, status, personality, appearance, plus everything about their lifestyle, from the type of car that they drive and the jobs that they have, to their hopes, desires and the things that they enjoy most. It's perfectly acceptable to stereotype here, as it's only an exercise and a means to an end.

And finally...

Now, on a fresh sheet of paper, produce a third and final list, identifying all of the assumptions that could be made about the advertising media itself. The creative brief will direct the choice of media, however there is plenty of scope to challenge the ways in which that media is normally used or perceived. For example, who said billboards had to be landscape format? Do they have to be seen from the front side only? Why are they nearly always flat and rectangular? Ooops – it looks like I've given you the first three assumptions for poster advertising, so I'll leave you to think of another 17 – you have less than 20 minutes, so you'd better get going!

Summing up

Once you've produced the three lists above you've completed the hard bit. Now all you have to do is to go through all of the 60 or so items on your list and challenge each one by asking: what if this isn't the case? You may be surprised at some of the lateral ideas that this may trigger and it's guaranteed to get the creative juices flowing.

In Chapters 1 and 2, we explored how the best ideas that are lodged in our subconscious rarely surface on schedule or when we're trying too hard. We've also seen the importance of stepping back from the problem to allow these ideas to incubate and finally emerge, and how there are numerous obstacles that can prevent you from having fresh ideas.

At your disposal are a range of creative techniques and approaches that can be used at various stages of the creative process to help loosen up creative thinking and enable you to generate ideas every time you get an advertising brief. In this chapter, you'll be introduced to a few of the most potent creative tools that you can use to stimulate lateral thinking.

Mind maps

Pioneered by Tony Buzan in the late 60s, mind maps have a wide range of uses from note-taking and organizing thoughts, through to mnemonic devices and systems for brainstorming. They normally take the form of a central word or concept around which linking thoughts and associations radiate in a branch-like diagram from the centre, exponentially growing outward with each branch or strand following its own conceptual theme or direction. A single branch can record an entire stream of consciousness triggered by the word or concept at the centre of the map. Mind maps enable an individual to capture their thoughts on paper to get a broader overview of inter-related themes and ideas. This can be a very useful device for advertising creatives.

Capturing ideas and associations

The most obvious way to use a mind map as a tool for stimulating ideas is to think of it as brainstorming on paper. As an advertising creative, you'll get used to exploring different ideas with a partner and bouncing them off each other. The benefit of using a mind map is that the two of you can capture every fleeting thought and random idea that pops into your head and you'll then have a better chance of exploring each of them in turn.

The first thing that you'll have to decide is what to put at the centre of your mind map. To begin with, I'd suggest that you use the advertising proposition or the key benefit of the product that you're advertising. This may involve re-writing it in a form that's short and snappy; something like 'lasts longer', 'tastes fruitier', or 'feels softer', for example. From here, you can start to map out the first thoughts or ideas that are triggered by this central proposition. These may be single words, phrases, images or complete ideas that come to mind.

On average, you'll probably want to start off with anything from four to eight of these surrounding the proposition. Collectively, these will establish your first layer of ideas, each of which will become an individual route to explore. Once you have this first layer of ideas in place, you can start generating more outer layers of your mind map by free associating from each of these ideas in turn, gradually growing the map outwards with each successive layer.

The best ideas are often triggered by very random thoughts and your mind map is a great way to capture those thoughts and to reflect on them

The best ideas are often triggered by very random thoughts and your mind map is a great way to capture those thoughts and to reflect on them. As you travel outward from the centre along a particular route, the ideas that you have are likely to become more divergent and their relationship to the central proposition more obscure. However, it's these ideas that are likely to be more novel and unexpected than the first thoughts that you had. Once you've developed one branch or strand as far as you can, start work on the next one, and then the next, until each of the routes that you initially identified have been fully explored.

Once your mind map is complete and you've explored each branch for potential solutions, start looking across the entire range of the mind map and try linking disparate ideas and thoughts to see if that leads you to any new solutions. You'll find that mind maps can be used in conjunction with a number of other techniques described in this chapter, which we'll explore as we go along.

Exploring different routes

As you start to explore a single branch or strand from the centre of your mind map, you should find that one idea will trigger another, which in turn will trigger another, and so on. Sometimes, the link between one idea and the next may be quite clear, whereas at other times it may be a little more abstract or in some cases an association that's uniquely personal to you. At this stage, remember not to try and judge whether the idea is going to work or not – just get it down on the page and see where it leads you!

It's really not important if the link between one idea and the next is ambiguous or something that only you really understand. The important thing is that each idea is triggered by a series of associations that are connected in some way to the central proposition, even though that connection may often be quite tenuous. Ultimately, it doesn't matter how, or by what route you get to your final idea, just as long as that idea provides a suitable creative solution to the brief.

Mind maps

Mind mapping

This mind map (right) charts out the various thoughts, associations and pathways that are being explored in response to a creative brief to advertise low-fat donuts. From amongst the many divergent ideas, a campaignable concept based on manipulated images of the product begins to emerge (below).

Mind map:
Suzanne Oke and Nik Mahon

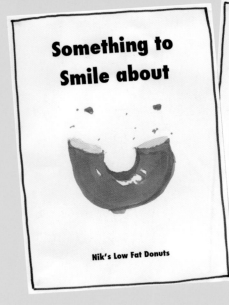

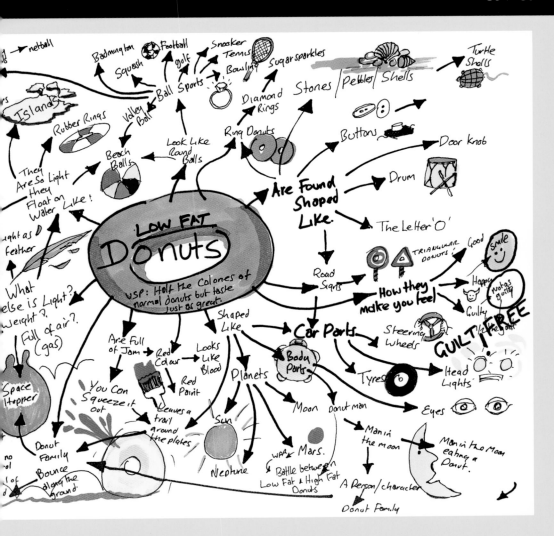

Consequences

Whilst it's important that your advert clearly communicates the brand proposition, this alone is not enough. You need to do this in a way that's personally relevant to your target audience. In order to do this, you need to go beyond the proposition to demonstrate what this really means to them. In other words, if the proposition is 'a richer-tasting coffee', you will need to demonstrate exactly how this can benefit the person who's reading your advert.

Right
Great Dane
Exploring the consequences of the advertising proposition can often provide ideas that are both lateral and witty – as seen in this advert for Eurocamp, which illustrates what happens when you holiday in a sunny place where your dog is welcome too!
Agency: BSL Group Unlimited
Client: Eurocamp

Extending the proposition

Within the creative brief, the proposition or product benefit is the first thing to look at or identify. In the best briefs, it will be clear and focused. In other briefs, it may be very general. In some cases, you'll have to extract one yourself from the rest of the text by reading between the lines or by making some assumptions based on the rest of the information that's given.

Once you've identified the proposition, start to extend it by asking yourself: 'what could this lead to?' So, if the proposition is 'our toothpaste makes your teeth whiter', look at the implications of this. It could mean that you acquire a more attractive smile, that your teeth appear brighter than anyone else's, or that other people will want teeth as white as yours.

You can then go further by looking at each of these consequences in turn and again asking the same question ('what could this lead to?') to identify further possible consequences. For example, if your teeth appear brighter than anyone else's, this could mean that everyone else has to wear sunglasses when they stand near to you, or that they're more reluctant to smile, or that any photographs depicting your smiling face come out overexposed.

The list of consequences resulting from this process can be endless and not every one of them will initially appear to offer a benefit. Some may appear ridiculous or even seem to provide more reasons *not* to buy the brand. However, as you know, now's not the time to assess your thoughts and ideas – it's just about having as many of them as possible.

Consequences

Discovering the 'real' benefit for the target audience

As one consequence can generate several others, you've probably already guessed that the best way to capture all of them is to use a mind map. Once again, start with the proposition at the centre of the map and then list a few initial consequences around it. It's then just a case of generating different branches of consequences from each one by using the same questioning technique described above.

Once you've fully developed all of the branches on your mind map, it's time to take a look at what you've got, and select the most promising consequences to pursue for a solution. The type of consequences that may provide you with the best solutions could be humorous scenarios, thought-provoking moments or simple snapshots of life. Either way, they should illustrate the proposition in a way that your target audience can relate to – something that resonates with their own experience.

Search each branch of your mind map for interesting consequences that may provide a solution. Let's see how this could work by taking a look at 'the toothpaste that makes your teeth whiter' example again. This could lead to you smiling a lot more. This could in turn lead to you appearing friendlier or more attractive. This could lead to you attracting more friends and company. This could give you greater self-confidence… and so on. You may then decide that you're not really selling 'toothpaste that makes your teeth whiter' (after all, that's just boring). What you're really selling is self-confidence!

The consequences of not having the product

A useful twist on this technique is to look instead at the consequences of not having the product. You can do this by using a mind map as before, but this time take any of the consequences from the initial mind map and reverse them to provide the central hub of your map. Returning to our toothpaste advert, for example, we could map out the consequences of having an unattractive smile, or teeth that are duller, or the kind of teeth that no one else would like.

You can then map out further consequences from each of these by asking the same question as earlier; 'what could this lead to?' You'll probably find that many of the consequences that you generate in this way will be opposite to those identified in your original mind map. One scenario could show someone who's reluctant to open their mouth to speak or smile. You can then ask yourself: 'how would they communicate?'; 'What would they do to distract attention from their teeth?'; 'How would other people react to them?' You can already see how these questions could prompt a humorous storyline for your advert or commercial.

Café
The consequences of wearing garments from the high-end London retailer, Harvey Nichols, is illustrated in a dramatically surreal interpretation of the term 'fashion statement'. In this menswear advert, women are literally bowled over by the effect.
Agency: DDB UK
Client: Harvey Nichols

Consequences

7

8

9

10

Gorilla

Global chocolate manufacturers, Cadbury, created a viral YouTube sensation with their original Gorilla ad, which spurned multiple remixes of it by the public. This commercial from the International Fund for Animal Welfare warns that 'a world without gorillas is closer than you think', by showing audiences what the iconic Cadbury's 'Gorilla' ad would look like without the gorilla. A thought-provoking message is produced that takes the viewer by surprise while providing a novel means of communicating the ecological consequences of mankind's actions.

Images: © IFAW/Rapp

Metaphors and similes

Metaphors and similes are really useful tools for communication that we tend to drop into everyday conversation on a frequent, and often automatic, basis. Phrases like 'as hot as hell' (a simile), 'as cool as a cucumber' (another simile), 'the tip of the iceberg' (a metaphor) and 'as fast as lightning' (simile) are all common examples. Using metaphors and similes enables us to communicate in more expressive terms and to emphasize certain aspects of what we have to say. More importantly, we can make a connection with the person we are addressing by using metaphors or similes that they can understand and relate to.

How advertising uses metaphors and similes

Metaphors and similes can be a great way to communicate a complex message or to demonstrate the operating principles of a product or concept that your audience may be unfamiliar with. By showing them something that they *are* familiar with, that's either similar to, or that operates on the same principle as the product (or an aspect of that product), your audience are more likely to connect with what you have to say and to gain a better understanding of the advertising message.

When a product has a certain property or quality that it needs to communicate through its advertising, a metaphor or simile can provide the perfect vehicle to achieve this. If the product is hard-wearing, for example, other things that have a well-known reputation for being similarly hard-wearing can be used to convey this message, often in a humorous fashion – a bruised and battered boxer after a prize fight, perhaps, or the shell on a tortoise, or an armour-plated tank.

Typically, the best choice of metaphors or similes is from those that exist in an entirely different field from the product that you're advertising

Brands that have a long-established or well-known proposition associated with their products can often get away with using metaphors or similes that are relatively cryptic, particularly if the adverts are part of a long-running campaign theme. A good example of this is provided by Volvo cars that, over the years, have fostered a reputation for quality-built cars with the emphasis on safety. In one particular advert, Volvo featured a photograph of an over-sized shark menacingly swimming in front of a group of divers who remain protected by a steel cage. Unlike many other print adverts for cars, there is no sign of the product in the advert itself, just the Volvo logo.

Constructing a metaphor or simile

The best way to start searching for an appropriate metaphor or simile is to first identify what it is that you want to say about the product. This will normally be the advertising proposition. Start listing all of the things that you can think of that involve the same concept or principle, or things that operate or function in a similar way. You can write these up as a list or, if you prefer, use a mind map.

The first layer of your mind map could be variations on the advertising proposition or different aspects of it. For example, if the advertising proposition states that the product is hard-wearing, you could also substitute this for 'tough', 'lasts longer' or 'robust'. Once you've identified the possible different variations or aspects of the advertising proposition, you can then start looking for alternative metaphors or similes that equally embody these qualities.

Typically, the best choice of metaphors or similes is from those that exist in an entirely different field from the product that you're advertising. So if you're producing a campaign for an inanimate object, such as a watch or the latest mobile phone, try using a living thing such as an animal or a person as your metaphor – and vice versa. This isn't a statutory rule, but it does seem that the most lateral solutions are those that are able to identify a connection or to create a link between the most disparate things.

Metaphors and similes

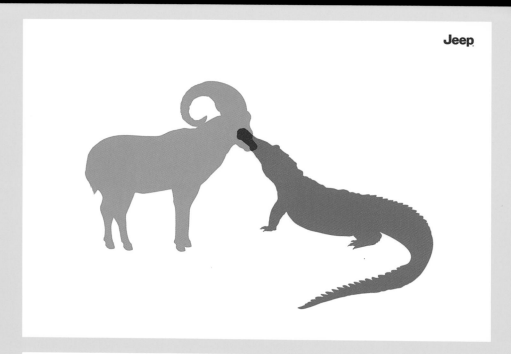

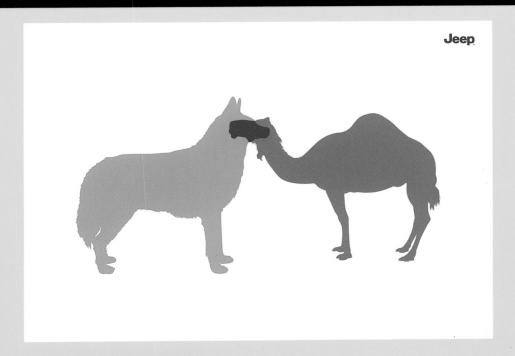

Visual metaphors

A clever combination of metaphorical images is used in each of these adverts to draw attention to the all-climate, multi-terrain, tough and hard-wearing qualities of the Jeep. The silhouette of a Jeep vehicle is subtly revealed in the area where the bushman and Eskimo, the husky and camel, and the mountain goat and crocodile meet.
Agency: BBDO/Proximity Malaysia

Checklists

We've already seen how the capacity to keep asking questions is vital to creativity and that questioning everything and challenging assumptions is a recurring necessity within most creative activities that require some degree of lateral thinking. However, in the rush to find an idea and to meet the deadline, it's often easy to forget this or to make do with the first idea that comes to mind. It's also sometimes difficult to know what kind of questions to ask. The following checklists can provide you with a series of prompting questions that can be adapted for the task at hand and utilized at various stages of the creative process. As such, they're one of the most useful creative tools that you can be equipped with.

Kipling's checklist

In 1902, Rudyard Kipling's *Just So Stories* were published, containing a poem that opened with the following lines:

*I keep six honest serving men
(they taught me all I knew);
Their names are What and Why and When
And How and Where and Who.*

Kipling's checklist presents us with six interrogative words (what? why? when? how? where? and who?) that we can systematically use to explore the advertising brief and all aspects of the brand, the brand message, and the target audience for that message. It's not only a useful tool for the creative team; it can be used by account handlers, media planners and other agency strategists to develop the creative brief and to make important decisions regarding the use of media, too. More importantly, it prompts you to ask all of the questions that you should be asking, but which may not otherwise occur to you.

The table opposite contains a few indicative examples of the type of questions that Kipling's checklist could prompt. It's a good idea to chart each of the six keywords as a separate branch on a mind map, enabling you to plot out individual questions that each one generates, together with any solutions as they present themselves. The questions that you ask will be dependent on the product and brief that you're working on, together with a variety of other circumstances that may be specific to your task and to the advertising objectives.

What?

What are we really selling or offering?
What do our target audience really want?
What problems or needs do our customers have?
What do they think of the brand?
What do we want them to think of the brand?
What do we want the advertising to achieve?
What are our competitors doing and what can we do differently?
What can we do to get people talking about the brand and to generate buzz?

Why?

Why would someone buy the brand?
Why wouldn't someone buy a different brand?
Why should they listen to what you have to say?

When?

When should we show the advert?
When should we show the brand being used
(past, present, future, on certain occasions, at certain events)?
When would you most rely on, or need the brand?
When would you least expect to see the brand?

How?

How do the target audience feel about this type of product or the brand itself?
How do the competition feel about us?
How can we best demonstrate the benefits?
How can we use the media in an unexpected way?
How do we show the product in a different way?

Where?

Where can we place the advert?
Where can we show or demonstrate the brand being used?
Where's the last place that people would expect to see the advert?
Where's the last place that people would expect to see the product?
Where's it most likely to perform best?
Where would people expect it to perform badly or fail?

Who?

Who are we really talking to?
Who are our competitors?
Who really loves the brand – and who hates it?
Who could we use or feature in the adverts?
Who would the brand be if it were a person?

Checklists

Demonstrating the proposition

How do you demonstrate the multi-purpose functionality of Volkswagen vans? The solution created by Brazilian agency AlmapBBDO was to print beer boxes, milk boxes and other relevant packaging with the vehicle image and livery.

Client: Volkswagen
Photographer: Mario Daloia
Studio: Daloia Estudio de Fotografia Ltda. São Paulo

Checklists

Don't
irritate
your new
boss.

Gentle and thorough cleaning for sensitive skin.

HARVEY NICHOLS
NOW OPEN IN BRISTOL
PHILADELPHIA STREET · QUAKERS FRIARS

Who do you use to sell the brand?
Who better to use than a baby for
Huggies' Gentle Care Sensitive
wipes (facing) and British animation
stars Wallace and Gromit (above) to
announce the opening of another
Harvey Nichols luxury retail store
in the UK?
Agency: DDB UK
Client: Harvey Nichols

Checklists

Osborn's checklist

Alex F. Osborn was an advertising practitioner who later became famous for pioneering brainstorming techniques. Osborn created a checklist of questions designed specifically for brainstorming sessions with the aim of generating new ideas from existing ones (opposite). Each of these questions can be used, one after the other, to push that idea further. You can use these questions in a variety of different ways when you're brainstorming advertising ideas. You can apply them to the product, the design of your advert, the media you're using or the advertising message itself.

When the advertising brief for the Yellow Pages telephone directory required the campaign to tell people how useful it was, the creative team decided to show it being put to another use (for something other than finding a telephone number) and showed a young boy using the directory to stand on (and thereby gain height) so that he could kiss his taller girlfriend under the mistletoe.

Another commercial for the directory showed an elderly man watching a TV film with his family. When the TV breaks down, he picks up the Yellow Pages, but instead of using it to find the phone number for a television engineer, he gives the television set one almighty whack with the directory, thereby bringing it back to life! What made these commercials so effective was the manner in which the storyline takes the audience by surprise. They communicate the advertising proposition in a totally unexpected way.

Can it be put to other uses?
Either as it is or modified
▼

Can it be adapted in any way?
▼

Can it be modified?
▼

Can it be magnified?
Made larger, longer, taller, have something added or be multiplied or exaggerated
▼

Can it be minified?
Made smaller, shorter, have something removed or reduced
▼

Can it be substituted?
Something or someone else, different elements, or other processes, approaches, places used etc.
▼

Can it be reversed?
Turned back-to-front, inside-out, roles reversed or turned into an opposite
▼

Can it be combined with something else?
Its purpose, its form or some other aspect of it

Petition

How do you show the difference that a signature on a petition can make? The WWF produced this poster in the form of a petition to support the Renewable Energy Bill – a piece of key legislation devised to combat global warming. As more signatures were added, the temperature in the thermometer-like pen could be seen to go down.
Agency: BBDO Guerrero Philippines
Art director: Joni Caparas
Creative director/Copywriters:
David Guerrero/Simon Welsh

Assumption reversals

One technique for challenging assumptions is to simply reverse them. To do this, you have to first spend some time identifying as many of these assumptions as possible – that's the difficult bit!

Identifying assumptions

The reason that it's so difficult to identify all of the assumptions that we could be making with regard to the creative task at hand is that much of what we know (or think we know) will be based on well-established mind sets that we are unlikely to be conscious of. To escape from these mind sets, we have to start questioning things that we could be taking for granted, and this can begin with the creative brief itself.

Whilst the brief sets out various mandatory criteria and parameters, together with other essential information that we can't choose to ignore, it's the way in which we interpret that information and apply our imagination that gives us greater scope to do something original each time. Start by breaking every aspect of the brief down into individual elements such as target audience, product, the media, the message, competitors and so on. Then, look at each element in turn and list as many assumptions as you can that you could be making about each of them – even if those assumptions seem quite logical, reasonable or scientifically proved.

Turning assumptions on their head

Once you've identified as many assumptions as you can, try reversing them. A good way to do this is to write out the assumption on a piece of paper as a short, single-sentence statement, such as: 'women love flowers'; 'men like football'; 'computers make our lives easier'; or, 'all puppies are cute'. Sometimes, these assumptions can be quite general or stereotypical in nature. On other occasions, you'll need to dig a bit deeper to identify the less obvious assumptions that you're making.

Then, all you have to do is to reverse the statement around, like so: 'women don't love flowers'; 'men don't like football'; 'computers don't make our lives easier'; or, 'not all puppies are cute'. In many cases, you'll create a statement that will sound illogical or nonsensical – but don't worry about this, just see where the thought takes you. Use the resulting statement as a provocation – something that's likely to stimulate springboard ideas or lateral solutions.

The rephrasing technique

This is a simple method based on the 'two-word technique' described by Arthur B. Van Gundy, Jr., in his book entitled *Techniques of Structured Problem-Solving* (1988). It works on the basis that different words can all have the same meaning, yet at the same time evoke different images, moods and associations. For example, the words 'organize', 'arrange', 'plan', 'design', 'prepare' and 'sort' could all be used in certain contexts to mean the same thing; however, each of us may have slightly different images or ideas that come to mind when we see or hear these words.

Using semantics as a tool for stimulating ideas

The first stage of this technique involves writing the advertising objective or proposition as a short, single-sentence statement that contains at least one verb, together with an adjective or a noun as key words. This may involve rewriting the proposition for the purpose of this technique. For example, if the advertising brief says 'tell the audience that we work harder to make sure that they're happy', the proposition could be written-up as: *'we work harder to make you happy'*. In this example, the keywords are 'work' (the verb) and 'happy' (the adjective).

The next stage is to rephrase this proposition statement in as many different ways as possible by substituting one or two of the key words within the statement with similar words or synonyms. To do this, begin by extracting the original keywords from the statement and against each of these words, list as many alternative words as you can (this is where a thesaurus will come in handy!). Alternative words for 'work' could be: 'labour', 'effort', 'slog', 'toil', 'try', 'operate'… and so on. Similarly, alternative words for 'happy' could be: 'content', 'joyful', 'gleeful', 'ecstatic', 'pleased' and 'glad'. Substitute these alternative words for the original keywords in order to rephrase the proposition statement in a variety of different combinations.

⌐⌐

Alternative words will have different connotations and degrees of emphasis, which will in turn stimulate different images and associations within your imagination

⌐⌐

The original proposition could be rephrased as: *'we do more to make you ecstatic'*; *'we labour harder to make you gleeful'*; *'we toil harder to make you content'* and so on, until you run out of alternative words and combinations. As you can see, most of the statements that you'll produce are likely to sound grammatically awkward or inappropriate; however, it's important to remember that you're *not* trying to craft a headline or slogan here. What you *are* trying to do is to prompt alternative ways of viewing the brand proposition, and a good way to start is to first verbalize it in a range of different ways. The alternative words will have different connotations and degrees of emphasis, which will in turn stimulate different images and associations within your imagination. Whilst the word 'work' may bring to mind an image of a stack of paperwork on an office desk, the word 'toil' may conjure up an image of a farm worker ploughing a field!

Like many of the other techniques described in this book, you'll find that this technique is most productive when used by a team – that's you and at least one other! This is because the technique is based on the different associations and connotations that alternative words may generate, and of course two different people are each likely to make their own different associations and connections, and see opportunities that their partner may have missed.

Once you and your partner have a whole range of alternative statements based on the advertising objective or proposition, start trying to imagine what each statement would look like if you had to visualize it in some way – try sketching it out as an image on paper and examine different ways of visually communicating what you have written. The more statements you've written the better, as you'll thereby have more material to stimulate your imagination.

Random stimulus and free association

One method of generating ideas is to use random stimulus (sometimes referred to as 'random input'). This can take the form of concepts, images, objects or words which, when selected by chance, are used to establish a connection with the problem itself. This compels the problem solver to approach the problem from an unconventional direction, thereby viewing it from a fresh perspective. In the context of a creative brief, random stimulus can be applied to either the advertising objective or the proposition, in order to approach the brief from a different route and so liberate new ideas.

Free association and forced connections

All creative problem-solving techniques involve some degree of free association and/or the capacity to establish 'forced' connections between disparate concepts, images, objects or words. Free association mimics the way in which our minds naturally wander from one thought to the next, linking each one seamlessly in a stream of consciousness that gradually takes us further from the initial thought or idea.

As human beings, we often tend to do this subconsciously without keeping track of every fleeting association that enters our heads (daydreaming is just one example of this). Mind mapping is an excellent way to capture many of those fleeting thoughts, as it can provide a tangible overview of the many different associative routes that we are exploring and also enable us to trace those thoughts back to the original thought or triggering stimulus.

As mentioned previously in this book, when presented with the same words, images or other forms of stimulus, different people will make different associations. This is because each of us, as individuals, have our own personal backgrounds, experiences, beliefs and levels of knowledge that enable us to see things in different ways from the next person. If this weren't the case, it would be a very dull world in terms of creativity and fresh thinking.

It also means that given the same problem or advertising brief to solve, it's possible for each of us to have a highly unique idea that is triggered by our own unique points of reference.

In contrast to free association, 'forced' connections are links that we are able to make between given concepts, images, objects or words. These links require conscious effort in order for us to establish them. For example, given a pencil (as either an object, a word or an image), the word 'mint' is unlikely to be the first thought that comes to mind. However, with conscious effort we *can* find a link between the two. How about a new product, for example – mint-flavoured pencils for people who like to chew their writing implements? This could lead to the idea of pens and pencils with different-flavoured ends. The concept of specially flavoured pens could be further extended to include scented pens with special calming, congestion-clearing or other aromatic qualities.

As a technique for generating ideas, random stimulus can employ the use of forced connections or free association in order to generate ideas or idea stimuli.

It's important to remember that ideas never happen in a vacuum. There's always something that triggers an idea; whether it's that television programme you saw the night before, a passing comment you overheard, or something you saw in the street

Ultimately, it doesn't really matter whether that great idea you had was as a result of free association or some forced connection that you made. At the end of the day, as long as something has triggered that idea, then that's all that matters.

Sometimes, it may feel as though the idea just sprang into your head 'out-of-the-blue', but it's important to remember that ideas never happen in a vacuum. There's always something that triggers an idea; whether it's that television programme you saw the night before, a passing comment you overheard, or something you saw in the street; there's never any creative output without input!

Random stimulus and free association

Using random stimulus

The use of any random stimulus is often most effective when the creative team has already spent some time brainstorming or discussing the brief and fresh thinking is needed. If words are to be used as random stimulus, then a means of selecting these randomly from an extensive list of common nouns needs to be chosen. The words could be written on cards or balls and drawn 'blind' from a box or bag, lottery style. Alternatively, you can use one of the many electronic random word generators that are available via the Internet – just type the words 'random word generator' into a search engine and take your pick!

Once you have your random word, write down all the thoughts that come into your head with regard to the word (it's important at this stage to put the advertising problem aside for the moment and focus only on your random word). Consider the properties or qualities of the object or thing identified by your random noun. Think about its function, how it works or operates, what it looks like, how it's constructed. Then try to use 'action' sentences to describe those things; for example, 'it has a shiny surface', 'it makes a loud noise that annoys people', 'it's made from lots of tiny pieces of glass that glisten in the dark', 'you have to wind it up to make it work' – and so on.

> **All that really matters is that you find a good creative solution that meets the requirements of the brief – how you get there isn't really important**

Write down each separate thought and association as a separate line and then, when you have at least a page of these thoughts, go back to the advertising brief and now write down how each of these thoughts could relate to the advertising message in some way. The connections you may find between the sentences on your list and the advertising message may be quite direct or something a little metaphorical.

Once again, the connections you establish could be very unique to your own personal way of thinking and to anyone else, they could appear quite cryptic or tenuous. All that really matters is that you find a good creative solution that meets the requirements of the brief – how you get there isn't really important.

The process of seeking connections between the random word and the advertising objective, proposition, or the product itself will enable you to view the brief from an oblique perspective and to find ideas which might otherwise have escaped you. In this sense, the random word becomes a trigger to stimulate lateral thought.

Random words
Students on the Advertising course
at Southampton Solent University in
the UK are shown here using their own
novel technique for randomly selecting
words to stimulate ideas.
Photographer: Nik Mahon

Random stimulus and free association

Here's how it works

Let's look at an example to see how this might work in practice.

Imagine that your client owns an international parcel delivery service and that the advertising brief requires you to tell consumers how reliable the service is. Now let's say that your random word is *'name'*. Your first thoughts might go something like this:

people have names
▼

pets have names
▼

names help us to identify things
▼

people can have lots of names
▼

some people change their names
▼

names can denote reputation and status
▼

songs have names
▼

book titles have names
▼

films have names…
▼

and so on.

The next step is to see how each of these thoughts could directly relate to an aspect of the product or advertising brief. Starting with the first thought (*people have names*), a question-and-answer approach can provide useful prompts and lead to a chain of consequential ideas, such as:

Question
What if parcels had names?

Answer
Each parcel could have its own name

Question
What could this lead to?

Answer
They'd each have their own personalities and feelings

Question
What could this lead to?

Answer
They'd start developing human traits, likes, dislikes and personal preferences

Question
What could this lead to?

Answer
They'd want to choose their own parcel delivery service.

This in turn could lead to your idea! This might be something like a commercial featuring parcels as individual characters who, given the choice, would choose your brand over the other, less reliable brands. The less fortunate parcels get upset, worried or anxious as they are left to be dispatched by another delivery service.

Once you've used your first thought to stimulate an idea in this way, move on to the next one and then the next, and so on, working through each of the initial thoughts that you listed and using them to generate ideas in a similar fashion. You can try this technique using random images or even random objects for stimulus, instead of words. If you're using a random object, try looking at its form and function when listing your initial thoughts. If appropriate, take it apart and look at how it works and its functional attributes. Is there perhaps a metaphorical link with the advertising brief at hand?

You may have noticed by now how many of the techniques that we've looked at use features from other techniques. You can see in the example above how random stimulus can involve elements from both Kipling's checklist and the 'consequences' technique that we explored earlier in this chapter.

Random images
Random images or objects can also be used to stimulate ideas.

The second-guess technique

Have you ever noticed how, whenever we listen to a storyline unfolding or an idea being presented, we tend to 'second guess' where it's leading or what the outcome is going to be. This is human nature and it stems from our compulsion to solve puzzles and make sense of any information that remains incomplete, even whilst that information is in the process of being communicated. We try to look ahead to see where the story or idea that's being described is going. This leads us to predict completely different outcomes or solutions from those that are eventually revealed by the original author of the story or idea.

Second guessing the idea

Incomplete or ambiguous information can be a powerful stimulus for alternative ideas. Whilst clarity and completeness are normally seen as positive attributes in relation to most aspects of communication, they also close down our options and tend to deter us from searching for alternative pathways or solutions. Leaving a story unfinished or only partially revealing an idea provides another person with the scope to take that storyline or concept in a different direction, thus resulting in alternative outcomes or solutions.

As an advertising team, one way that you and your partner can harness the creative potential of second guessing is to use the second-guess technique to push each others' individual ideas in different directions. First, spend some time on your own, each brainstorming a few initial ideas in response to the brief that you're working on. Next, present these to each other in a format that only partially begins to reveal the directions that each of you are exploring, or that may just hint at your respective solutions in a rather oblique or abstract way. Then, see where you can take or develop each other's ideas, prompted by the thoughts or directions that have already been initiated. There's a good chance that each of you will have ideas or solutions that are different from your partner's, and may even be better!

There's also no reason why you can't partially present your ideas to a much larger team of individuals to see where they can take it. The more people involved in this process, the more alternative ideas you're likely to generate!

Where's that idea heading?
When we listen to someone describing
an idea, we tend to jump ahead
and try to predict or 'second-guess'
where that idea is heading. In doing
so, we often discover other ideas
and solutions from those that were
originally intended.
Photographer: Nik Mahon

Morphological analysis

Earlier in this book, we explored how the act of combining disparate objects or concepts to find new ideas and solutions often characterizes the creative process. In many cases, this is achieved instinctively and sometimes, by random chance; however, there is also a systematic means by which many more opportunities to discover new combinations can be identified and fully explored. This is called morphological analysis.

Morphological analysis involves first identifying as many different aspects and components that might form part of the solution, and then mixing and matching these components to generate or stimulate novel ideas that may otherwise be overlooked

Using a matrix to explore different combinations

Morphological analysis involves first identifying as many different aspects and components that might form part of the solution, and then mixing and matching these components to generate or stimulate novel ideas that may otherwise be overlooked.

The first stage is to create a morphological matrix. Take a look overleaf to the matrix on page 114 to gain a sense of what one looks like and how it works. Then, start by drawing out a grid of squares (about 10 × 10 to begin with). You can hand draw this grid or produce it on a computer and print off as many as you like, just as long as each square is large enough to accommodate a simple thumbnail sketch or drawing.

Next, above the top line of the grid, title each vertical column with a component that is likely to be an aspect (or part) of any solution to the advertising brief at hand.

For example, if the brief is for a building society savings account and the advertising message is 'it's more flexible than other accounts, giving you greater freedom without the normal limitations and restrictions', then there are a variety of different components that could form part of your campaign. Some of these may relate to savings accounts in general, such as *money*, *security*, *banks*, *growth* and *accumulation*. Others may relate to the benefit itself, such as *freedom* and *flexibility*. You should also use components that oppose these benefits, such as *restriction* and *rigidity*.

Once you have a series of columns, each entitled in this way, you should start filling in each of the squares below each component with any related images or thoughts that enter your head. So, for the column entitled *banks*, you might have images of coins, banknotes, cash machines, safes, pinstripe suits and bowler hats, for example (yes, you are allowed to use stereotypes here!). For the column entitled *growth*, you may have images of trees, plants, charts and graphs, upward-pointing arrows, an adult and child, or a bottle of fertilizer. Similarly, for the column entitled *freedom*, you may have an image of broken chains, the cut strings of a puppet, a hole broken through a prison wall, a bird flying in the open sky or even an image of the Statue of Liberty. The column entitled *restriction* may contain images or thoughts that conflict with these, such as a pair of handcuffs, someone tied up in knots, prison bars, the inside of a prison cell, a straitjacket or a caged bird, for instance.

Sometimes, an unusual combination of just two or three images or thoughts that you've identified will be enough to stimulate an idea

Once each of the columns has been filled with as many related thoughts and images as you can readily identify, the real fun begins! Start looking across the matrix that you have created and try combining images or thoughts from different columns together to see if that triggers an idea or prompts a solution to the brief. You don't have to try and combine images from every single column on your matrix. Sometimes, an unusual combination of just two or three images or thoughts that you've identified will be enough to stimulate an idea.

Morphological analysis

MONEY	SECURITY	BANKS	GROWTH	FREEDOM	FLEXIBILITY

The morphological matrix

A morphological matrix like this (above) enables you to explore different, interesting and unusual combinations. Images from this matrix can be combined to prompt ideas such as the solution visualized on the opposite page (right).

Group brainstorming

The term 'brainstorming' has been used to describe a variety of different group idea-generating activities, ranging from two individuals bouncing ideas off each other in a bar, to the more formal structure of a brainstorming meeting between a collection of individuals where a facilitator will guide the process and different routes and ideas will be mapped out and collated on flip charts, boards or walls.

'Piggy-backing' and bouncing ideas

Group brainstorming, even in an informal fashion, can provide a powerful source of ideas, particularly if individuals or creative teams have already had an opportunity to produce some initial ideas on their own, and so already have some starting thoughts or concepts to present to the larger group. It's often the case that other people within the group will be able to see something in your idea that you may have missed or overlooked. When it's your own idea, you're likely to be so close to it that you can easily miss the obvious.

In a larger group, when someone spots something that you've missed and points out that 'you could do this with your idea…', it's not long before someone else in the group will add 'yes, and if you do that… you could then do this…', and so on. Suddenly, you'll find members of the group are piggy-backing off each other's ideas and observations, and interesting ideas start bouncing back and forth as fresh ones emerge. In this sense, the group become larger than the sum of their parts, enabling something that may have started out as just a vague direction or incomplete idea to grow wings and fly!

It's important to bring all of your ideas to a group brainstorming session – not just the ones that you think are any good. Even the wildest and most inappropriate ideas may trigger a better idea from someone else, and so these sessions require a certain degree of mutual trust within the group, based on the understanding that no one is going be embarrassed or humiliated by any other member of the group… even though some of your ideas may raise some laughs!

When conducted as part of a group critique session, brainstorming around initial ideas that have already been presented can generate further ideas, as individuals reveal those they may have second-guessed during the presentation of the original idea (see the earlier section on the second-guess technique).

Brainstorming
A brainstorming group can often take your initial idea and push it further by identifying opportunities that you may have missed or by discovering alternative directions that could be usefully explored.

Case study ● The Toyota iQ launch

Launching the iQ microcar

Finding a unique and novel way to demonstrate the product benefit or brand proposition, in a manner that engages your target audience, is a fundamental part of the creative process. When the car manufacturer Toyota wanted to launch their new model, the iQ microcar, they briefed Belgian advertising agency Happiness Brussels to communicate the 'exclusive agility' and control of the vehicle. The iQ incorporated a unique front wheel differential design that gave it a turning radius of only 3.9 metres, just over half that of a London black cab – renowned for its ability to turn tight circles. The target group for the advertising was to be 18–35-year-old urban people.

It would have been relatively simple for the agency to have demonstrated the iQ's amazing manoeuvrability and steering capacity by showing images of the car being driven around town, negotiating tight bends, tiny parking spaces, and seemingly impossible turns – however, that would have been just a little too obvious and would have merely echoed the type of advertising that many other car manufacturers were producing at the time.

Happiness Brussels

Happiness Brussels chose to look at the more unusual *consequences* of having a car with this type of advanced precision steering qualities. They explored how these qualities could be demonstrated and underlined in an unconventional manner that would capture the imagination of the target group.

The solution involved creating an entire new type font from A to Z, based on the movement of the car when filmed from above by a camera mounted to a crane. This collaborative project involved Happiness Brussels recruiting typographers, a software designer, and a European GT3 racing champion, Stef van Campenhoudt, as 'font driver'.

Four coloured dots affixed to the corners of the car were recorded by the aerial camera which tracked every movement of the car in real time and then sent that information to custom software developed by interactive artist Zachary Lieberman. This software allowed the path of the car and the skids it created to be mapped out and eventually converted into typeforms.

Typographers Pierre and Damien from Pleaseletmedesign briefed the driver on the type of skids that they required to create the strokes from which they could then develop the font.

A short video documenting the process was distributed online and pointed viewers to the Toyota website, at the same time inviting them to download their free copy of the new iQ font and to book a test drive of the car. The video was subsequently featured on over 6,000 influential design, technology and automotive blogs and received considerable global attention both on- and offline. The iQ font was downloaded over 24,000 times from the Toyota website.

The iQ font project
The branding project for the Toyota iQ involved a team of professionals from a variety of different fields and disciplines: advertising, design, typography, interactive art, software development and GT3 Racing, resulting in the first type font to be created by a car!
Art Director: Tom Galle
Creative Director: Gregory Titeca
Copywriter: Ramin Afshar
Head of Art: Cecilia Azcarate Isturiz
Typographers:
Damien Aresta and Pierre Smeets
Creative Managers:
Karen Corrigan and Gregory Titeca
Software Developer:
Zachary Lieberman
Advertising Agency:
Happiness Brussels
Design Studio: Pleaseletmedesign
Account Director: Pascal Kemajou
Client: Toyota Brand: iQ

Hello I'm the iQ font

abcdefghijklmnopqrstuvwxyz
ABCDEFGHIJKLMNOPQRSTUVWXYZ
0123456789
. , : : | ? + = @ & ( ) /– # " "

Lorem ipsum dolor sit amet, consectetur adipisicing elit, sed do eiusmod tempor incididunt ut labore et dolore magna aliqua. Ut enim ad minim veniam, quis nostrud exercitation ullamco laboris nisi ut aliquip ex ea commodo consequat. Duis aute irure dolor in reprehenderit in voluptate velit esse cillum dolore eu fugiat nulla pariatur. Excepteur sint occaecat cupidatat non proident, sunt in culpa qui officia deserunt mollit anim id est laborum.

Case study ● The Toyota iQ launch

Creating the iQ font
A sophisticated tracking system
mapped out the movement of the
Toyota car to create the new iQ font.

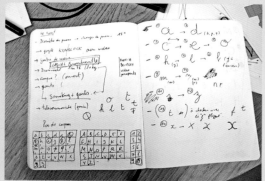

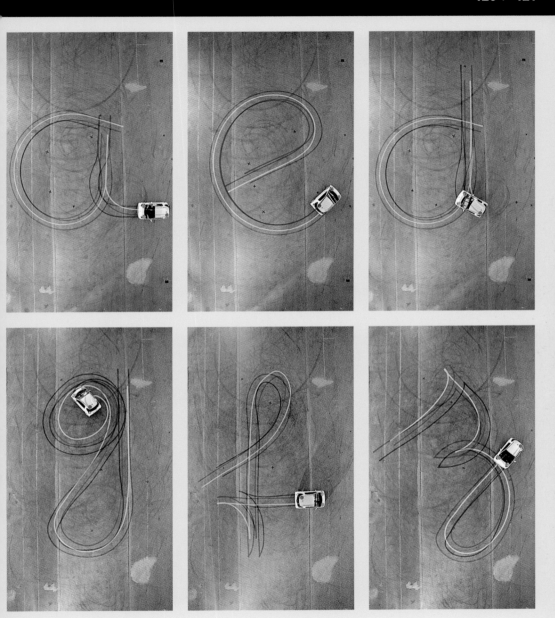

Give it a go ● Focusing on the proposition

Face the consequences

Here's an exercise that will help you to identify alternative reasons why someone may want to buy your brand, and thus enable you to develop a more interesting, original and compelling advertising idea. Before having a go at this, it's worth taking another look back at the section within this chapter entitled 'Consequences' on pages 82–87. Then choose one of the following propositions:

● 'Your clothes will feel softer with Caress fabric conditioner'

● 'Aspreze Extra tablets will make your headache disappear faster'

● 'Cool Cats – the most comfortable shoes you'll ever wear'

● 'You soak away all your worries and troubles in an Oasis bubble bath'

● 'Snippers – the cheapest haircuts in town'

● 'Glucojuice – the drink that gives you more energy'

Start listing all of the direct consequences of the benefit offered by that proposition. For example; what would happen to you as a direct consequence of wearing the most comfortable shoes in the world... or having much more energy after a glass of Glucojuice? What could this lead to? List as many consequences as you can think of, and then start looking at what the consequences of *those* consequences could be.

Once you've identified an entire second generation (or layer) of consequences, then start looking at the possible consequences of *those* consequences to create a third generation of consequences, and so on, until you've exhausted all of the possibilities you can think of.

The chances are that you'll have identified several alternative and interesting benefits that are a little more novel and unexpected than those normally associated with the product.

One tip might come in useful here! Starting with the central proposition, you'll find that a mind map will provide you with the best means of recording and exploring all of the different pathways and layers of consequences.

Interrogate the proposition

Choose one of the propositions listed in the preceding exercise and use the questions outlined earlier in Kipling's checklist to prompt ideas. Taking the 'Oasis Bubble Bath' proposition, for example, ask: who would really need to soak their worries and troubles away? What worries and troubles would they have? Where (or in what circumstances) are they most likely to have worries or troubles? When are they likely to be most worried or troubled? Why are they worried or troubled? How did they get this way and how do they feel after an Oasis bath?

These are just a few examples of the questions that you could ask. I'm certain that you can think of more! Once you've interrogated the proposition in this way, look at the answers that you have to each of the questions and see if any of them suggest an interesting angle or scenario for an advert or commercial. Try this exercise for each of the listed propositions and see how you get on.

Summing up

Both of these exercises involve applying a questioning approach to the proposition. With some advertising briefs, where the proposition may be more abstract or complex than those provided here, you may need to rephrase the proposition in a way that enables you to apply the consequences technique or Kipling's checklist simply and effectively.

Now that we've explored a few
of the tools and techniques for
stimulating ideas, this final
chapter takes a look at an array
of approaches that can be used
in the execution of those ideas.
These general approaches
range from the use of reframing,
humour, shock and sex, to
provoke a reaction and trigger
a variety of emotional responses,
to product demonstrations,
comparisons, testimonials,
challenges and tests that can
engage your audience and
provide a powerful foundation
on which to base your idea.

Reframing

One thing that's common to some of the best advertising around is the element of surprise. Advertising that catches us unawares, or contains within it some kind of unexpected twist tends to be more memorable and in most cases entertains or amuses us – which is always a good thing! One way in which advertising achieves this is through the use of 'reframing'. Reframing is the means by which a piece of advertising will initially lead the audience to think one thing, and then proceed to reveal a completely different message as further information is introduced. In effect, it confounds the audience's expectations.

Confounding the audience's expectations

In order to create surprise, an advert first has to get the audience thinking in a particular way or direction. It does this by initially presenting information that enables the recipient to establish a frame of reference – a familiar context in which to place that information. In other words, as part of the advertising audience, we link that information to what we already know or believe by referring to our past experiences or current knowledge and beliefs. We do this in order to try and make immediate sense of the information we're presented with. Then, once we think we know what we're looking at, we're presented with further information that changes the context completely, and in doing so, changes the meaning of the message.

To confound the audience's expectations, the creative team must first have a good understanding of that audience, and the manner in which they are likely to interpret what they see or hear in the advertising

To confound the audience's expectations, the creative team must first have a good understanding of that audience, and the manner in which they are likely to interpret what they see or hear in the advertising. The use of stereotypes in advertising can make the reframing process simpler, as they tend to trigger a predictable response or interpretation from a wider audience.

When we see certain images or situations that we are familiar with, we tend to assume a certain scenario or outcome. It's then relatively simple for the advertiser to overturn that assumption by presenting us with further information that is contradictory to our initial understanding and forces us to reinterpret what we see or hear.

For example, when we watch a scene showing a man stumbling down a street and speaking with a slurred voice, we're likely to assume that he's intoxicated. As the storyline unfolds, and more information is revealed, it may then transpire that he's actually suffering a stroke, or some other illness; our initial assumption is overturned.

It's relatively easy to see how this can be accomplished with time-based media, such as television or radio, where the reframing element can be introduced towards the end of the commercial, but with print-based media where all the information is visible at the outset, it can be a little more difficult. The secret remains in creating a strong visual hierarchy whereby the eyes of the audience are initially led through each visual element of the advert in a pre-determined sequence. This sequence first enables them to contextualize and interpret the information, and then introduces information that challenges or conflicts with this interpretation to completely change the meaning or turn the story around.

Humour

Humour is one of the most popular approaches used in advertising today. If an advert entertains and makes you laugh, it's almost certain to make you feel good about the brand that it's advertising. Not only that, it tends to make the advertiser seem more 'human', so it's particularly useful when the product or service concerned is one that has a reputation for being very serious, austere or is generally suffering from corporate facelessness. More importantly though, humour provides you with an excellent opportunity to connect, engage and interact with your audience at an emotional level.

What makes people laugh?

Much of the humour we see used in advertising employs the reframing model we have just examined. By using familiar storylines, scenarios or images that enable the target audience to establish a frame of reference or context for what they see or hear, the advertiser can then disrupt that frame of reference with a comic 'twist' – something unexpected that's introduced within the advert or commercial that changes the context in a humorous way. This is how the punchline of a joke works. Alternatively, humour can also be derived from situations that *prevent* the audience from establishing a frame of reference until the introduction of a final piece of information. In this case, the audience have to construct a frame of reference retrospectively, which subsequently enables them to make sense of everything else leading up to that point.

One great source of humorous material is human behaviour itself, particularly if that behaviour is something common that's recognized by most of your target audience. It's what comedians call 'observational humour'. It resides in our nature to act or respond in predictable ways to certain situations which, when replayed to us out of context or with some degree of exaggeration, can seem comical or hilarious. Start observing the ways in which people generally behave or react in particular circumstances and the type of behaviour that's common to most of us. Look for things that we've all experienced or can relate to in some way that may provide fertile material for comedy.

No Nonsense

In this commercial for John Smith's beer, British comedian Peter Kay enters his dog for a top dog show. It competes against trained pedigree champions by simply fetching a newspaper for its owner, aptly demonstrating the 'No Nonsense' concept behind the campaign.
Agency: TBWA London
Client: John Smiths

Different styles of humour

There are a variety of different styles of humour that can be used in advertising. There's humour derived from socially taboo subjects such as death, illness, morality and sex. Tackling these issues can often create a tension between the subject area and the message that you want to express. By treating them in a playful yet sympathetic manner you can relieve that tension with laughter. In this way, 'blue humour' (sexual innuendo or references of a sexual nature) or 'black humour' (typically referring to 'dark' subjects, such as death) can provide a great way of connecting with your audience with plenty of creative impact.

Another style of humour exploits the comedy of mishaps or mischance. Unfortunate circumstances that befall a character either through an accident of their own making or resulting from a series of events can turn a serious situation into a comic one. This is where your product can feature – perhaps as a remedy or preventative solution. There's also crazy or zany humour. Often used for brands aimed at youth markets, it normally has a viral quality that is readily absorbed into popular culture.

Try adapting a joke or comic situation for your product. Think about how you can link that comic situation to a proposition. Is the situation a result of the product's properties in some way? Does it happen because someone drinks Heineken… or because someone wants people to think he owns a Mercedes? How have the properties of the product or service affected the behaviour of the person in your advert?

Shock and sex

Shock advertising is designed to create a strong impact and is often used for the purpose of shifting deeply embedded beliefs or for bringing important issues to the attention of the audience in a manner that may change their behaviour or prompt them to think more deeply about something. Shock advertising manifests itself in a variety of different forms, ranging from campaigns that tackle taboo or socially sensitive subjects, to those which may depict disturbing or unpleasant images, or use explicit language to grab our attention.

The effects of shock advertising can vary enormously from simply making people feel a bit uncomfortable, to being deeply distressing

When to shock your audience

The use of shock is undoubtedly an effective means of grabbing attention. The effects of shock advertising can vary enormously from simply making people feel a bit uncomfortable, to being deeply distressing. Before employing it in your advertising, you have a responsibility to take into consideration its appropriateness in terms of the level of shock you plan to deploy, with regard to the nature of the product, the message, the context and the target audience themselves – how will it affect them?

During the 80s and 90s, the Italian photographer Oliviero Toscani produced a series of print-based advertising campaigns for the fashion company Benetton. These campaigns depicted controversial images, ranging from those that were mildly provocative to some that were deeply disturbing (depending on your own point of view and sensitivity to such things). The adverts covered issues such as racism, child labour, birth, death, execution, AIDS, war and human rights, and in most cases featured reportage-style photographs from agency stock.

One thing that appeared to fuel the widespread controversy and moral debate that ensued was the fact that it was the first time that a large corporation had been seen to use such images to sell their products. Many of Benetton's campaigns at this time highlighted human differences that separate rather than unite people and, as such, became a means by which the company sought to foster social cohesion and tolerance through its brand, the United Colours of Benetton. The company justified their strategy as one that did not set out to shock, but one that was rather designed to communicate.

There is, of course, the question of just how effective shock advertising is when audiences can very quickly become desensitized through over-exposure to such material. Prolonged campaigns that employ ever-increasing levels of shock are often required in order to sustain the desired effect

Charity, public health and welfare advertising

Charity and public health or welfare advertising often employs shock advertising in order to grab attention on a minimum budget in an area that's very competitive and where it's often difficult to motivate audiences to act or respond in the desired manner. There is, of course, the question of just how effective shock advertising is when audiences can very quickly become desensitized through over-exposure to such material. Prolonged campaigns that employ ever-increasing levels of shock are often required in order to sustain the desired effect. Advertisers also have to consider the long-term issue of how the consistent use of shock advertising may affect the way in which consumers perceive your brand.

Shock and sex

Lungs

This campaign utilized the cigarette bins that have appeared across London since the UK smoking ban was introduced in 2007. These became billboards for posters based on chest X-rays showing the lungs of a smoker being gradually filled with cigarette butts and ash, designed to shock smokers with a graphic depiction of what they are doing to their own lungs.

Agency: Saatchi & Saatchi London
Client: QUIT

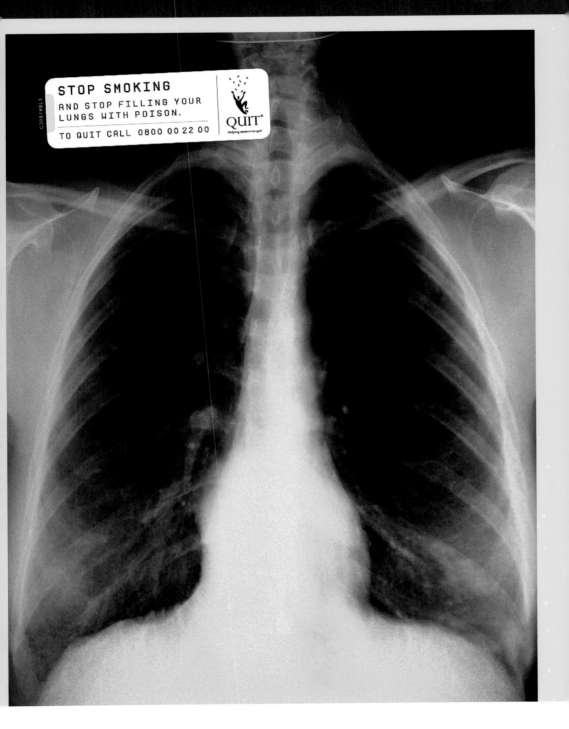

Shock and sex

Photography © Mat Baumer

NZ Transport Agency and NZ Police
New Zealand Government

Sleep before you drive

Left

Creek

This advert was part of a campaign created for the New Zealand Transport Agency, showing an authentic reconstruction of a fatal crash caused by fatigue, but which replaces the smashed car with a smashed bed, and carries the copyline 'sleep before you drive'.

Agency: Clemenger BBDO
Client: The NZ Transport Agency
Photographer: Mat Blamires
Images: © NZ Transport Agency

Right

Condom strips and plastic surprises

Shock can be presented in many different ways and forms. In this campaign for Surfrider Foundation (a non-profit environmental organization dedicated to the protection and enhancement of the world's waves and beaches), actual garbage found washed up on beaches was packaged to resemble seafood and was then displayed at a local farmers' market. The packages were also photographed for a print-based campaign.

Agency: Cobleigh Productions
Client: Surfrider Foundation
Art director: Matt Cobleigh

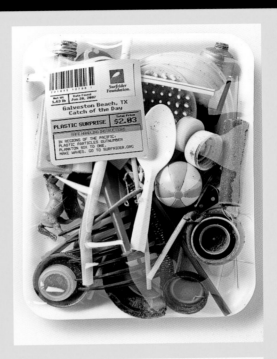

Shock and sex

Different types of shock

There are four broad areas in which shock advertising can be categorized, which we shall explore in further detail below.

Tackling the taboo

Shock advertising tackles taboo subject areas or sensitive issues such as sex and sexuality, religion, death, illness, disability, abuse, violence, racial or cultural differences and social or moral conflict. Typically, these are subjects that people may feel uncomfortable discussing.

Using explicit language

The second area is using explicit language, lewdness or profanity within the advert to grab attention and create shock. In some cases, expletives may be suggested or hinted at within the advertising. The FCUK campaign produced for French Connection UK is a good example, as are the many occasions where letters may be substituted for asterisks to suggest a certain word that may be found offensive or too vulgar when printed in full.

Using upsetting imagery

The third category of shock advertising includes all adverts that depict horrific, terrifying, repulsive or simply upsetting images to provoke a reaction. Certain health-warning adverts, such as those used to warn consumers about the risks of smoking or drug abuse, have, together with road-safety commercials, been at the forefront of advertising campaigns that attempt to shock audiences into changing their behaviour.

Similarly, charity organizations such as Amnesty International, WWF and Barnardo's have traditionally used such images to depict or suggest the horror of a reality that many people would choose to ignore, or remain oblivious to.

Shocking with facts

The fourth category is using facts or statistics to shock audiences. The fact that they are *facts* can make them even more shocking as they can also appear more authentic in many ways. Here are a few examples: *'Every day, four children die in the US due to abuse or neglect'*; *'10,000 teens are infected with STDs every day'*; *'Since 1600, more than 700 species of plants and animals have become extinct'*; *'Over one billion people in the world live on less than one dollar a day.'* When accompanied by the right kind of image, such facts can be extremely thought-provoking and compelling.

You should be aware that it's not always a case of what you show, but what you choose not to show that can have a greater shock effect. Sometimes, planting an image in someone's head (as opposed to actually showing that image) can be more powerful. Images that implicitly suggest the horror that you are referring to, rather than explicitly showing it, can sometimes affect your audience at a much deeper personal level.

Sex sells

Throughout the history of advertising, brands have used sex to sell. This has ranged from the use of sexy male and female models or celebrities, to more explicit visual or verbal material that invariably generates controversy and can raise complaints. In terms of marketing techniques for grabbing attention, the use of sex in advertising is unrivalled: the sight of a pair of long legs on a billboard or a well-toned torso on the page of a magazine is more likely to capture our gaze than an image of the latest iPhone – even though that's likely to be quite sexy as well!

Campaigns can vary from those that use double entendre, innuendo or suggestion, to those that are much more overt in their use of sexual imagery or language. There are certain products or issues that are readily associated with sex, and others where the links are more tenuous or cryptic. Whilst lingerie, perfume and fashion products may have obvious associations, less obvious are the associations between sex and cars, chocolate or ice-cream – all products that have used sex in their advertising.

Harnessing desire

In these more abstract examples, the common link is desire (and in some cases guilty indulgence). The sexual undertones contained within the iconic ad showing an attractive young woman seductively peeling the wrapper off a Cadbury's chocolate Flake bar before slowly nibbling away at it were not lost on many. A decade or so later, Häagen-Dazs launched a campaign featuring images of scantily clad young couples enjoying a tub of ice cream as a prelude or accompaniment to sex – pitching the brand as a guilty pleasure on a par with sex itself.

When to say no

Although the use of sex in advertising can be a highly effective strategy for grabbing attention and drawing interest, it also comes with a high degree of risk. There's a big risk that it may offend or outrage a large section of the population. There is also the risk that negative publicity can affect sales and damage brand reputation. Brand owners have to look beyond just the short-term impact of a campaign and consider the long-term effect on the brand and the future development of its marketing strategy.

It is important that any references to sex or sexuality are relevant to the brand or the brand message, and that care is taken not to cause unjust offence or reinforce negative stereotypes such as those associated with gender roles and sexuality. As with all advertising that features taboo subject areas, some of the best campaigns actually challenge such stereotypes.

Shock and sex

Above
AXE wake up
To encourage young guys in Japan to use AXE deodorant as part of their daily routine, a 'wake-up call' in the form of a beautiful woman reminding them to use the product could be downloaded as a video alarm clock message to their mobile phones.
Agency: BBH Singapore
Client: AXE
Images: © Unilever Japan

Right
Couch fcuk and table fcuk
These adverts produced by the Miami Ad School Madrid present a raunchy visual representation of the fcuk brand name in a cleverly amusing fashion that alludes to the provocative nature of the acronym.
Creatives: Regis Pranaitis, Franciso Arranz, Rafa Martinez – Miami Ad School, Madrid

Playing with type and wordplay

Typography can establish the tone of voice expressed by a campaign and, although its use may be quite subtle or understated, it can also be used as a major visual feature in the headline. Whilst the visual aspects of typography can be exploited to help communicate the brand message, so too can the verbal aspects of the language itself. Clever use of double meaning and wordplay can enable reframing and add to the memorability or creative impact of an advert.

Right
Wordplay
To promote their new free-range butter, Anchor employed double meanings and a twist on a popular phrase ('home sweet home') in this campaign, to communicate the message that their dairy cows are free to graze outside in fields all year round.
Art director: Dave Masterman
Copywriter: Ed Edwards
Designer: Kylie McLean
Agency: CHI & Partners
Client: Anchor
Images: © 2009 CHI & Partners

Words as images

In a traditional print-based advertising campaign, the headline and image need to work together in a way that one gives meaning to the others so that the two components come together to communicate a particular message. It's quite often the case that one component will reframe the other by changing or shifting the context, thereby changing the interpretation of the message – creating a 'twist'. In some cases, the headline can be the image itself, or at least part of it. For example, it could be an image of a piece of signage in which the text becomes the headline; or the typography could be constructed from parts of the product or from items related to it.

Make sure that by choosing to feature a type-based image in your campaign you are doing so in a way that is relevant to and that enhances the advertising message and so adds value to the campaign. At the end of the day, it's important that your creative use of typography isn't just a clever trick that gets in the way of the real message.

Playing with type and wordplay

Double meanings and puns

Understanding the complexities and subtle nuances of language, and the different ways in which it can be used as a tool to confound, surprise and engage your audience, is a vital skill for crafting advertising headlines or copy in general.

Different languages will have their own peculiarities and anomalies that can be exploited in their own individual ways to create sentences or phrases that can have more than one meaning (depending on the context), and enable reframing to occur. In such cases, a single element within the advert, such as the image or the logo, can give a headline a completely different meaning from the one that may first be interpreted on the initial reading. Of course, the one over-riding limitation of such headlines is that they are often language-specific, and in that sense they do not readily lend themselves to international campaigns.

Generally speaking, as an advertising student you should avoid the use of puns in your headlines. Creative directors tend to see a lot of pun-based adverts in student books, most of which are inappropriate and have little real relevance to the advertising message or product benefit.

Right
Roger More
Puns are generally frowned upon by many advertising creatives. However, now and then they can work really well, particularly when used in an amusing way that fits the tone and 'voice' of the brand. The pun works well in this advert for Durex Performa condoms, which are designed to prolong sexual performance. The colloquial language in the copyline refers to an actor who played the role of the notorious womanizer James Bond in the well-known movies.
Agency: McCann Manchester
Client: Durex
© McCann Manchester

Having said that, the playful use of a word in two different senses can sometimes be a very effective way of reframing – just make sure that it's also relevant!

Be aware of the difference between a clever use of wordplay that makes the message clearer or more memorable, and the use of a bad pun that tends to feel and sound like one of those terrible jokes that most people groan at. The worst kind of puns are those that use words that are similar in sound but different in meaning, particularly if those words are also spelt differently in the first place. A prevalent use of puns in your headlines is unlikely to impress the advertising agencies and senior creatives who will be viewing your book.

Demonstrations and comparisons

'Seeing is believing', and so one of the most convincing ways of getting your target audience to believe what you have to say about the brand is to show the brand in action. In some cases, this may involve demonstrations of how well the brand performs in certain challenging conditions or circumstances, and in other cases, it may involve demonstrating how the brand out-performs its competitors, often by direct comparison.

Showing the product in action

It's not enough to make an amazing claim about your brand. You actually need to back it up with some credible evidence! Back in the 80s, when Araldite wanted to show just how strong their glue was, they used the glue to cement a car to a billboard, accompanied by the headline: 'It also sticks handles to teacups.' Although only a single billboard site was used, the dramatic nature of this stunt generated considerable impact and word-of-mouth interest, particularly when Araldite mounted a second car on top of the first, with the headline: 'The tension mounts!' Demonstration techniques such as this, where the brand is pushed to its limits, are often referred to as 'torture techniques'.

Sometimes, the benefits of a brand are a little more difficult to demonstrate, but the key is to find a dramatic or unusual way to underline that benefit in a manner that's believable. All you need is a little imagination. When Honda wanted to demonstrate how reliable their cars were they ran a commercial that featured individual components of a disassembled Honda Accord vehicle, knocking or nudging each other in an elaborate domino-effect sequence to activate a precisely planned chain reaction between each of the components, that finally triggered a model of the new car to roll down a ramp whilst the voiceover declared: 'Isn't it nice when things just work.'

You should consider the different ways in which you can demonstrate your product. It may be something to do with its appearance, or its performance. It could equally be about the reactions it causes, or the effects it may have on someone's behaviour, personal characteristics or abilities. Think about where you can show the product in action, where it is most likely to perform at its best, or conversely, where it is most likely to fail or perform badly. You can show the brand operating in extremely unfavourable conditions or alternately encountering difficult challenges and succeeding.

Emergency
When your client's an image bank, what better way to promote their services than to demonstrate exactly what you can create with their images?
Art Director: KC Chung
Copywriter: Eddie Azadi
Executive Creative Director: Graham Kelly
Account Director: Jun Shea
Art Buyer: David Chan
Agency: TBWA Tequila Singapore
Client: Photolibrary

Demonstrations and comparisons

Left
Torture test
To prove that Breeze Excel washing powder removes tough stains in one wash, the product was wrapped in a white T-shirt and mailed to women's groups across Thailand. By the time the parcels reached their destination, the T-shirts were badly soiled, so recipients had to wash them with the sample to make their T-shirt look new again.
Agency: Lowe Bangkok
Client: Breeze

Below
Whopper virgins
This Burger King ad shows taste tests carried out in the remotest parts of the world where participants had never tasted a burger; here they tested to see which tasted better – a Whopper or competitor's burger.
The BURGER KING® trademarks and images are used with permission from Burger King Corporation.

Matching the brand against its competitors

Some major brands will, on occasions, demonstrate their benefits by comparing themselves to their competition. This is particularly true when you have two major brands, such as Microsoft and Apple, McDonalds and Burger King, or Coca-Cola and Pepsi-Cola competing for poll position as brand leader. This type of comparison advertising can use a variety of different techniques, ranging from taste tests and challenges that make direct references to a competing brand, to those that make a more discreet or veiled reference to a competitor, sometimes hinting at the brand name concerned, with an oblique reference to their advertising images or marketing claims.

Caution must be exercised in making sure that any claims or statements you make, particularly with regard to the competition, are accurate and defensible. You should also be aware that by initiating such a campaign, you can expect a counter-campaign from the competition that you are, in effect, attacking. During the 60s, in the USA, the competition between the leading car rental company Hertz, and their closest competitor Avis, came to a head when Avis launched an advertising campaign claiming that because they were 'number two', they tried harder, providing examples such as cleaner ashtrays and more reliable service in general. Although they didn't mention Hertz by name, the inference was clear. Hertz eventually hit back with a campaign that attempted to highlight all the reasons that Avis were only 'number two'.

Comparing the brand to something else

Comparing your brand to something else can be an effective means of communicating the positive benefits or advantages that the brand offers. In many cases, this will involve the use of a metaphor, or the allusion to something that is similar in nature or form. In the previous chapter, we explored how useful metaphors can be as a means of establishing a connection with the audience, and in order to express a complex message in a simpler, more engaging fashion. Sometimes the comparison is embedded in the brand name itself; 'Velvet' toilet paper, 'Monster Munch' crisps, or the 'Jaguar' car, for example. When you compare your brand to something else, either directly or indirectly, you have an opportunity to associate your brand with the same qualities, properties or characteristics that are inherent in that thing.

Demonstrations and comparisons

The rose campaign

This ambient poster for the diamond jewellers, De Beers, was displayed in New York's Grand Central Station. It used 25,000 red roses to spell out the words 'A diamond is forever.' As the roses wilted and died, it demonstrated the temporary nature of other romantic gifts and added new meaning to the term 'killing off the competition'.

Agency: JWT
Client: De Beers
Images: © De Beers

Engaging the audience in your campaign

The best advertising engages its audiences to varying degrees and levels. New media technology has enabled advertisers to interact and engage with consumers in a manner never before imaginable. However, the power of traditional media to make a connection on an interactive level shouldn't be underestimated. These days, the combination of new and traditional media channels as part of a broader integrated marketing campaign provides advertisers with greater scope for cutting through the noise and establishing stronger relationships with their customers.

Puzzles, conundrums and teasers

Many of us enjoy doing puzzles and solving playful problems or riddles. Whether it's the newspaper crossword, a sudoko, a guessing game, a murder mystery or a jigsaw puzzle, at one time or other we've all engaged in some kind of puzzle-solving activity for personal enjoyment, recreation or satisfaction. It's also a human trait that we don't like to leave questions unanswered or problems unsolved. In order to make sense of any information we are presented with, our minds will always strive to find answers and solutions to such questions or problems. This is why advertising that presents the audience with a puzzle or conundrum to solve has the ability to engage that audience in a much deeper way than advertising which adopts a more passive style of communication. While individual consumers spend time trying to solve that puzzle, there's a good chance that the brand itself is on their mind and settling in their subconscious.

Teaser campaigns are created to prolong audience engagement and interaction by presenting extremely abstract or cryptic advertising messages or oblique references that, at the outset, may offer very few clues as to the identity of the brand or the advertising message. As the teaser campaign rolls out, more clues are presented until eventually all becomes clear and the brand or its message are revealed.

"

Teaser campaigns are created to prolong audience engagement and interaction by presenting extremely abstract or cryptic advertising messages or oblique references that, at the outset, may offer very few clues as to the identity of the brand or the advertising message

"

Challenges and tests

A sure way to engage your audience is to set them a challenge or test. These can range from commercials for food and drink brands that challenge you to taste the difference between their product and their competitors, to 'test yourself' type ads that offer you a chance to test your skills, abilities and a variety of other personal attributes, such as employability, health and fitness, creativity, intelligence or even life expectancy (as once used by a life insurance company).

Most of us enjoy pitting our wits against something or someone else, particularly if we can do so in a manner that spares our embarrassment should we fail or perform badly! Advertising that provides this opportunity has a good chance of engaging your audience at a highly interactive level.

This is particularly true if the challenge or test is linked to some kind of response mechanism, such as a phone number or online address that consumers can use to forward their answers or results to and subsequently receive some form of feedback or other 'reward' from. It's also a great way for brands to open up a dialogue with the target audience.

The 'challenge' doesn't always have to incorporate any particular level of difficulty. It may simply be a prompt to get the recipient to do something that involves an element of interactivity, such as: 'Try this today...' or 'Type something in the box above...' or 'Click anywhere on the screen...' The provision for consumers to interact with the brand to discover something, or to simply be entertained, helps to establish a stronger bond between those consumers and the brand in question. Ultimately, if people like your advertising, they tend to like the brand as well or to 'buy into' the brand message. Make sure that the manner in which you choose to engage the audience or that the nature of the interactivity has some kind of relevance to the brand message or the advertising proposition itself.

Engaging the audience in your campaign

The UN voices project

This direct poster campaign for the United Nations engaged members of the public by inviting them to use their mobile phones to photograph the mouths of the people featured in each advert, and to then send the photograph to a given number. The sender would then receive a recorded message telling the story of that person in their own words and voice.

Agency: Saatchi & Saatchi Sydney
Client: United Nations
Executive Creative Director:
Steve Back
Copywriter: Steve Jackson
Art Director: Vince Lagana

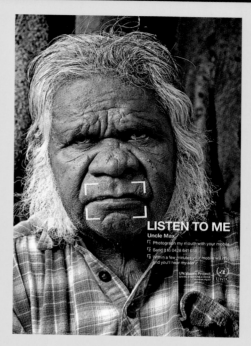

LISTEN TO ME
Uncle Max

1. Photograph the person's mouth with your mobile.

2. Send it to the number on the ad.

3. Almost instantly your mobile will ring and you'll hear their story.

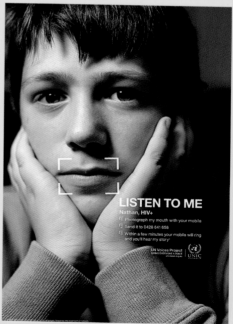

LISTEN TO ME
Nathan, HIV+

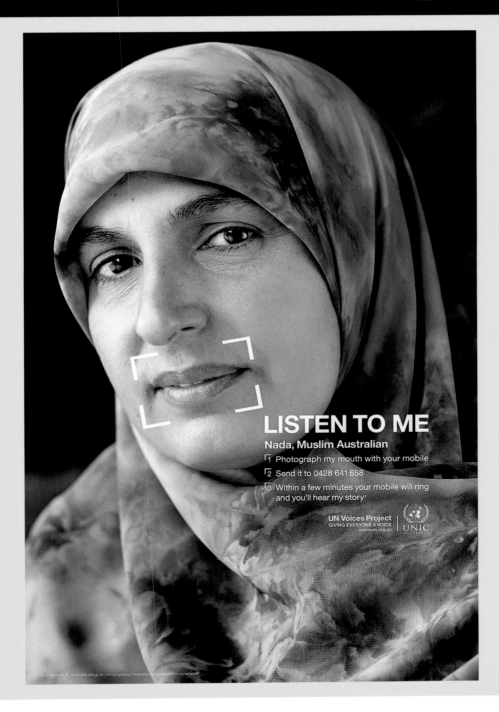

Exaggeration

We've already looked at a number of ways in which advertising can grab attention, create impact, generate interest and engage with the audience. Another way is through the use of exaggeration, either in terms of physical size or scale, or in terms of the type of claims that you make about the brand.

Go large!

One means of grabbing attention in a dramatic fashion is to take everyday images or objects from real life and to show them larger than life in your advertising. By showing an ordinary image or object in an extraordinary way, you're likely to get people talking – and your advertising could quickly go viral. Of course, it's essential to link such a strategy to the advertising message or proposition. So if you're advertising a clothes store for larger size men and women, for example, you may perhaps hang a gigantic suit or dress from the side of a tall building accompanied by the name and logo of the store. Alternatively, you could announce that your particular brand of potato crisps now comes in a larger king-size pack, by having a giant crisp-bag-shaped, helium-filled balloon, strategically placed to float above key city centres.

Exaggerate

'Going large' in this way will of course make your advert more noticeable; but better still, it's a means of telling people that your brand is bigger, larger, and more spacious, or that it covers more ground or offers more than its competitors. It doesn't always have to be an image, an object or the brand itself that you're depicting large scale. It can instead be a claim that you make about the brand, or what you show the brand accomplishing that is larger than life. Similarly, it may be the scenario itself that you exaggerate, often to achieve a comic effect or create a humorous situation. You can show the kind of things that can happen as a result of having (or not having) the brand.

For the sake of humour, these things can often depict unbelievable scenes that may, for example, show people achieving amazing feats because they ate a particular brand of breakfast cereal, drank a particular brand of beer, or used a particular brand of body spray! This is fine just as long as you're not making explicitly false claims that your audience are likely to believe to be true. The intention here should be to entertain your audience, not to deliberately fool them.

Bigger storage ideas

To promote the fact that IKEA produce practical boxes and drawers in all shapes and sizes for all storage needs, advertising agency Ogilvy Frankfurt redesigned the front of a whole apartment building in one of Frankfurt's busiest streets. Giant size mock-ups of IKEA storage boxes were turned into attention-grabbing balconies, boldly targeting people living in small flats and apartments with the advertising message.
Client: IKEA Deutschland GmbH & Co. KG
© Inter IKEA Systems B.V.

Experts and invented characters

Testimonials or endorsements from experts, professionals, celebrities or even fictional characters can add credibility to your advertising claims and help to define the character of the brand itself. There are, of course, a lot of factors to consider when choosing a personality for this purpose, and the greater the level of involvement that he or she may have with the brand, the greater the risk. If the chosen personality is to become the 'face' of the brand, then you must be certain that their character fits well with the brand personality and that the association will have sustained longevity. It's important that the chosen character is favoured and well liked by the target audience, and is unlikely to fall out of favour during their tenure.

Use an expert witness to present your case

Expert witnesses can vary from well-known celebrities, to unknown professionals or individuals who have subject-related experience or well-informed opinions on issues related to the product or brand message. Their positive testimonials or endorsements can add weight to your argument and help to substantiate any claims that the advertising is making about the brand or service. When using well-known celebrities, there is always a danger that they could fall from grace with the target audience and consumers in general – or worse still, do something to embarrass the brand.

❝

Brands that are represented in their advertising and marketing communication by famous celebrities tend to be perceived as having the same kind of personality, ideals and values as that celebrity

❞

As most consumers are aware that celebrities and any other expert witnesses receive substantial fees for providing such endorsements, there is also a risk that consumers may believe that they're only extolling the virtues of the brand because they're getting paid to do so.

However, the benefits of celebrity endorsement can outweigh the risks. For a start, it's an easy way to quickly express a brand personality, particularly if the brand is new or relatively unknown. Brands that are represented in their advertising and marketing communication by famous celebrities tend to be perceived as having the same kind of personality, ideals and values as that celebrity. Celebrity endorsement is also a great way to target certain markets. All you need to do is to select a celebrity who's popular with that target group, is respected and who appropriately reflects the brand personality.

Personifying the brand

You don't have to use real living people or existing fictional characters to endorse or represent the brand. You can invent a new character. In this case, there will be no fees to pay your character, and they're unlikely to get involved in any embarrassing or inappropriate activities that would be certain to generate negative publicity for the brand! Better still, you have complete control of what they say and do, and over how they look and behave. They can be human, animal or even alien!

So whether it's Betty Crocker, a jolly green giant, a panda bear or a Martian robot, the use of created characters as a personification of the brand can be an attractive proposition. It also provides advertisers and their agencies with the flexibility to modify that character over time, and to reflect current styles and fashions in a manner that's relevant to the brand and its audiences. There is also greater scope to use your character across a variety of different media from traditional billboards and press adverts to online commercials and guerrilla marketing stunts, as the character can be created with this in mind.

Even more creative approaches

Now that we've looked at some of the most useful approaches, creative strategies and routes that can be adopted as a means of communicating an advertising message, here's just a few final ones that are worth mentioning. *Topicality* allows you to tap into current issues or events that are of interest, whilst *parody* enables you to emulate the style and fashion of other adverts or well-recognized visual material to inject some humour into your campaigns. Lastly, *viral advertising* can enable the brand message to be carried much further, with relatively little media spend.

Guerrilla advertising stunts and ambient media have great potential to go viral the minute that they have people reaching for their mobile phone cameras to take photos and send them as picture messages to friends or family

Topicality

References to current issues, events or newsworthy stories are a good way of borrowing interest from current affairs in a topical and attention-grabbing fashion. In most cases, this involves subverting the news in a humorous fashion. Chances to react to unexpected events that make the news are fleeting, and require agencies and their clients to recognize such opportunities and seize them fast. In some cases, pre-scheduled events that make the news headlines, such as celebrity weddings, sport tournaments and government elections, can allow you ample opportunity to prepare ahead of time. However, some of the cleverest ideas are based on topical events or stories, which provide you with little opportunity to spend a week or so brainstorming or exploring different creative routes. Many of them are impromptu moments of creative wit and genius that can give you a bit of an edge on competing brands.

Parody

Parodies and spoofs can be an excellent way to invest humour into your idea. You can mimic a certain style of advertising or a particular advert or commercial. This is often funniest when the product or brand that you are mimicking has very little in common with your own brand and would normally use a completely different style of advertising. You can also parody material from cinema, television, literature, art, design, music, sport or politics – anything from typefaces and logos, to musical themes and cartoon characters.

Iconic images, well-known scenes or styles of advertising that are well recognized by your target audience provide the best material for parody. In order to do this well, it's important to have good references for the original material that you are parodying. It's essential to identify the key features that give the original material its distinctive visual style and personality. Then you need to accurately emulate these features, ensuring that any changes you make, such as the inclusion of your own brand, fit with the visual style of the original.

Viral

Throughout this book, you've read fleeting references to viral advertising. Any advertising images or clips that are passed on from one person to another, by whatever media, which have the potential to exponentially spread to even larger groups of people, are considered to be viral. However, in order to achieve this, the recipients have to first feel the desire or compulsion to forward the advertising to a third party. It has to entertain or inform them to such an extent that they can't help but want to show it to a friend or acquaintance. In many cases, it will be something humorous or witty that they wish to share with another person.

The media that's used can also affect the viral nature of the advert. Social networking sites, email and mobile media lend themselves to this as word of mouth travels fast via media channels such as these. Guerrilla advertising stunts and ambient media also have great potential to go viral as soon as they have people reaching for their mobile phone cameras to take photographs and then send them on as picture messages to their friends or family. It's easy to see why viral campaigns are such an attractive option for advertisers. They not only offer the free use of media channels, but they can also reach an extremely large section of your target audience in a relatively short time.

Even more creative approaches

boys and girls

true or false?

34

Here is Jill talking
to Katie.
"I hear you and Andrew
are doing it," says Jill.
"If you want any advice,
or anything, you can
talk to me."

key word

advice

38

Tam and Kirsty walk through the park.
They see Anne-Marie sitting on the roundabout on her own.
She's holding an empty bottle and she's covered in her own vomit.

Using pastiche
Produced in the style of the classic Ladybird titles of the 1950s and 1960s, these two books produced on behalf of NHS trusts in Glasgow, Lanarkshire and Ayrshire mixed the innocence of the original children's books with West Scottish dialect and sexual content to stimulate discussion amongst children aged 12–16 on issues such as peer pressure, bullying, boasting and lying in relation to sexual matters.
Agency: GRP Glasgow
Client: NHS
Images: used with permission of GRP

34

Tam and Kirsty meet and kiss.
"Kirsty," says Tam.
"You're right. We should wait until we're ready."
This makes Kirsty very happy.

key word   ready

Case study ● James Boag's Great Tasmanian Pipeline

The Great Tasmanian Pipeline

Whilst the rise in digital technology has driven the development of new media channels through which to communicate the advertising message, those new channels are only part of a much broader array of media options that are available. Using a variety of different media will not only increase the opportunities you have to reach your target audience, it can also strengthen the overall impact of the message. A multimedia campaign that utilizes both new and traditional media in a synergistic fashion can often have an effect far greater than the sum of its parts. Beyond this, today's major brands have to consider how their advertising campaign will integrate with their other marketing communication such as design and public relations.

Developing the campaign idea

A campaign that demonstrates the effectiveness of a truly integrated marketing strategy employing a range of different media, was the one produced for James Boag's Draught Beer in 2008. The brand is a well-known and respected name in brewing, however, outside its native Tasmania, relatively little was known about its draught beer. The aim of the campaign was to launch the brand in mainland Australia, with the message that it was now available on tap with that 'just poured' draught taste. At the same time, the brand owners Lion Nathan wanted to underline the beer's Tasmanian heritage and brewing credentials.

The central campaign thought was of the beer being pumped directly from the brewery in Launceston, Tasmania, across the Bass Strait directly to mainland Australian bars and pubs via a fictitious pipeline. The concept was brought to life through a public awareness campaign that first informed Australians about the plans to build 'The great Tasmanian Pipeline', and then kept them updated with its progress.

Constructing the pipeline

Images of construction workers laying gigantic sections of green pipe were seen on posters together with ambient installations of the green pipeline which were placed on location at various bars and out on the street. To make the idea even more convincing, official-looking public notices regarding the pipeline work were posted in and around towns where the pipeline was due to be installed and flyers were handed out on the street notifying people of the work that was supposedly being undertaken.

Trucks conveying large sections of the distinctive pipeline were to be seen driving in and around cities. Various other media stunts, together with targeted emails, a Facebook group and a series of rich media banners leading consumers to a dedicated website created by Publicis Digital, helped reinforce the whole concept in a tongue-in-cheek fashion. The website featured online consumer promotions, product give-aways and a pipeline project manager who provided information on the pipeline through a series of newsfeeds, updates and videos which included footage of the pipeline construction.

Generating buzz

The simple but original idea at the core of this campaign provided the brand and its communication agencies with plenty of creative scope. The tone and style of the material entertained and engaged consumers in a positive 'feel good' manner and generated a great deal of 'buzz'.

According to Micah Walker, Mojo Sydney Creative Director:

The Great Tasmanian Pipeline idea is a simple, unexpected way to give the arrival of Boag's Draught on the mainland some news and talk value.

The idea of beer literally linked and pumped from its source straight to your local, and all of the project detail around it – from construction films and notices to actual physical pipes and pipe workers – just reinforces Boag's commitment to bringing you great beer.

Case study ● James Boag's Great Tasmanian Pipeline

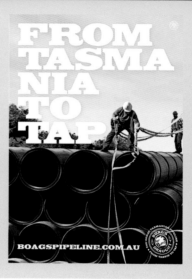

The Great Tasmanian Pipeline

This elaborate integrated marketing campaign for James Boag's draught beer drew together advertising, design and public relations in a manner that generated maximum media exposure and buzz.

Lion Nathan
Category Director: Arno Lenior
Marketing Manager: Raniero Miccoli
Brand Manager: Richard Spicer

Publicis Mojo
Account Director: Simon Ludowyke
Creative Director: Micah Walker
Art Director: Paul Sharp
Copywriter: Mike Burdick
Digital Art Director: Andy Cooke
Creative Services Director:
Lisa Vermaak
Senior Producer: Oscar Birken
Senior Digital Producer: Julia Prior
TV Production: Penny Brown

Zing
Account Director Offline PR:
Mike Maurice
Account Director Online PR:
Sean O'Byrne

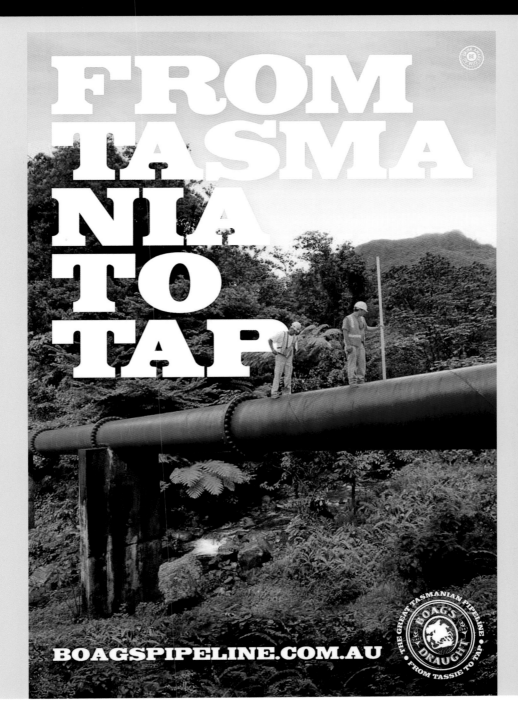

Give it a go ● The idea notebook

Building up your notebook

Your ideas notebook should also be a repository for observations or insights you could have at any time. You may not be able to find an immediate application for every thought, idea, insight or observation that you have in his way, but by gradually adding more material to your notebook, you will eventually create an important source for ideas and inspiration each time that you have a new advertising brief to work on.

Look for comic moments that could possibly be adapted in some way to add humour and wit to an advertising idea that you may have at a later date. Look also at human behaviour and the way that people react in certain situations – could that behaviour be attributed to a particular product or service perhaps? Look for stereotypes, visual clichés and other material that can trigger mind sets and help you to introduce an element of reframing within your idea.

Capturing your ideas

You can have an idea anytime and anywhere; the only thing that's certain is that you can't be certain when or where you'll have it. The important thing is to make sure that you have a means of capturing your ideas as and when they emerge. Start to keep an ideas notebook to hand, something that you can easily carry around with you wherever you go. Your ideas can manifest themselves in a variety of different ways. Sometimes they may be ideas for adverts and at other times they may be more abstract – not so much solutions but random thoughts that you may find interesting.

Summing up

All of these things should be captured and recorded in your notebook, then when you have a substantial collection of material in it, you can start to look for opportunities to use that material for advertising ideas. It could, over time, become the first place that you look for inspiration whenever you commence a new project.

Developing your curiosity

Earlier in this book, we looked at how important it is to be curious and keep asking questions. Your notebook can be a good place to develop your curiosity. Each time you start work on a new brief you should spend time trying to identify as many questions as you can about the product or brand, such as: How does it work or function? How is it constructed? Can it be used in some other way? What would someone who'd never seen anything like it before think it was?

Where possible, use doodles, sketches or photographs to explore different answers to those questions and, in no time, your notebook will gradually become the central hub of your thoughts and ideas. Remember, the key to having creative ideas is to ask lots of questions. The difficult bit is knowing which questions to ask!

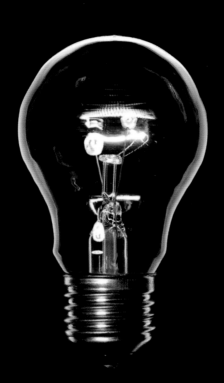

A great idea can come to us at anytime and anywhere – often when we least expect it, and regardless of whether or not we are focused on the specific problem at hand at that particular moment. As with all forms of creativity, none of the 'rules' are set in stone and our most creative moments can sometimes occur when we decide to break the rules or turn them on their head.

It's often a case of throwing out everything that you know (or think you know) about the brand and the task at hand and discovering a new way of interpreting the problem. One way of doing this is to think like a child again. As children we constantly question the way things are, and then as we grow older, we tend to ask less of those questions. To find lateral solutions we first need to identify all of the things that we may be assuming about the given problem, and then challenge each one to see where it leads us in terms of new ideas and fresh thinking. We need to learn to become curious again.

Asking lots of questions and interrogating the brief further, is just one way to open up your thinking and have fresh creative advertising ideas each time. Here are a few of the other methods that we've examined in this book:

● Re-interpret the problem – finding new ways to see problems can lead to fresh ideas. Are you trying to solve the right problem?

● Every so often, try breaking your normal routine – everything from your daily schedule to the way that you tackle creative problems.

● Don't be afraid of exploring alternative routes for no particular reason other than the fact that they look interesting! If you already know it's going to work, then you're not going to produce anything new. Try out different things, take a risk and experiment.

● Be eclectic in drawing inspiration from different sources. Read books you wouldn't normally read, see films you wouldn't normally watch, listen to music you wouldn't normally hear and try to experience things outside your general field of preferences.

● Have lots of ideas for each brief and don't be too fussy at the outset as to if they'll work or not – judge their value once you have a stack of them. Remember: quantity equals quality and for every 100 ideas you have, you may create one or two 'gems'.

● Have wild ideas as well. Try using creative thinking tools and techniques to generate unusual or provocative ideas as well as the more usual or acceptable ones. 'Crazier' ideas can often provide a stepping stone or springboard to a highly original, workable solution that no one had considered before.

● When you're tackling a creative brief, take a look at what the other products in that category are doing, then do the opposite in a way that both fits the brand personality and supports the advertising message.

● Finally, start collecting and capturing material in a notebook: odd ideas, observations, personal insights, interesting images, humorous moments and shared human experiences that encompass a range of emotions. Look at what makes people laugh, cry, get angry or curious. The key to communicating with an advertising audience is to demonstrate empathy with them, and to do this you first have to understand common aspects of human nature or experience that they will all relate to.

Bibliography

Paul Arden
Whatever You Think, Think the Opposite
Penguin
2006

Chris Baréz-Brown
**How to Have Kick-ass Ideas: Get curious,
get adventurous, get creative**
Harper Element
2006

Pete Barry
**The Advertising Concept Book –
A complete guide to creative ideas,
strategies and campaigns**
Thames & Hudson
2008

Rob Bowdery
Copywriting
AVA Publishing
2008

Ken Burtenshaw, Nik Mahon, Caroline Barfoot
**The Fundamentals of
Creative Advertising**
AVA Publishing
2006

Tony Buzan
**The Mind Map Book –
Unlock your creativity, boost your
memory, change your life**
BBC
2010

D&AD
D&AD annual

Edward de Bono
Lateral Thinking: A textbook of creativity
Penguin
2009

Jean-Marie Dru
**Disruption: Overturning conventions
and shaking up the marketplace**
John Wiley & Sons
2006

Jean-Marie Dru
**How Disruption Brought Order:
The story of a winning strategy in the
world of advertising**
Palgrave Macmillan
2008

Steve Harrison
How to Do Better Creative Work
Prentice Hall Business
2009

Tom Himpe
**Advertising is Dead –
Long live advertising!**
Thames & Hudson

Gavin Lucas, Michael Dorrian
**Guerrilla Advertising –
Unconventional brand communication**
Laurence King
2006

Nik Mahon
Art Direction
AVA Publishing
2010

Marty Neumeier
**Zag: The number one strategy of
high-performance brands**
Peachpit Press
2006

Mario Pricken
**Creative Advertising –
Ideas and techniques from the world's
best campaigns**
Thames & Hudson
(revised edition)
2008

Luke Sullivan
**Hey, Whipple, Squeeze this –
A guide to creating great advertising**
John Wiley & Sons
(3rd edition)
2008

David Trott
Creative Mischief
LOAF Marketing
2009

Arthur B. Van Gundy Jr.
**Techniques of Structured
Problem Solving**
Van Nostrand Reinhold
(2nd edition)
1988

James Webb Young
A Technique for Producing Ideas
McGraw-Hill Professional
(new edition)
2003

Jurgen Wolff
**Creativity Now: Get inspired, create
ideas and make them happen – now**
Prentice Hall Life
2009

Here are a few approaches, techniques and terms that you've already encountered in this book – with a brief reminder of what they are.

Assumption reversals

A process that involves first identifying assumptions that are being made about a specific problem (or an aspect of that problem), and then challenging each of these by reversing them or assuming the opposite.

Brainstorming

Popularized by Alex Osborn in the 50s, brainstorming is a term more generally used to describe a group activity whereby individuals collectively generate a large quantity of ideas in order to find a creative solution to a specific problem.

Consequences

An idea generation technique that involves looking beyond the product benefit to identify the possible consequences of that benefit, in order to understand the real reason why someone would be interested in the brand.

Convergent thinking

The process of focusing down to start analysing, assessing and evaluating the ideas generated during the preceding period of divergent thinking, in order to filter out the best solutions.

Divergent thinking

The period of open, unrestricted lateral thinking where judgement is deferred and ideas are generated, with the emphasis on quantity, rather than the quality, of those ideas as solutions.

Free association

The process of linking thoughts, ideas or words one by one, in a seamless stream of consciousness that leads thinking beyond the initial stimulus, thereby enabling us to make new connections.

Ideation

Quite literally, the process of idea creation.

Kipling's checklist

A checklist of six key questions: Who? What? Why? When? Where? And how? Each of these can be used to systematically explore and interrogate the brief, and to generate a range of different ideas and solutions through a questioning approach.

Lateral thinking

A term coined in the 60s by Edward de Bono to describe a way of thinking that employs unconventional techniques and approaches for disrupting logical thinking and breaking routine patterns of thought to find alternative ideas and solutions.

Mind mapping

A technique pioneered by Tony Buzan which involves mapping out ideas, insights, thoughts and associations as a series of pathways or branches as they radiate outward from a central question, image or problem, and examining the relationships between the different words and images on the map in order to discover new ideas or solutions. Mind maps can also be used in a variety of other ways to plan, record, categorize or prioritize information.

Morphological analysis

A systematic technique that employs a grid system (morphological matrix) to identify the various components of a problem and to then rearrange and recombine those components in novel and original ways to discover new ideas, solutions, opportunities and possibilities.

Osborn's checklist

Devised by Alex Osborn, this checklist is comprised of a series of questions that can be used to examine how the problem, advertising message, product or service can be viewed differently or modified in some way to provide a fresh perspective and to trigger alternative ideas.

Random stimulus

A method for idea stimulation that involves the random selection of concepts, images, objects or words which are then introduced to the problem-solving activity or brainstorming session to prompt ideas or move the process further on towards a creative solution. The random stimulus introduces a disruptive element to the process, which compels individuals or groups to tackle the problem from a different direction.

Reframing

The process that occurs when an element of the communication, such as a headline or an image, changes the way in which we interpret that communication. Our initial ideas about what's going on in the advert shifts dramatically as we look more closely. Reframing is deliberately engineered to create surprise.

Rephrasing technique

A technique that involves rephrasing the creative problem by first articulating that problem in a single sentence or phrase, and then rewriting that sentence by substituting key words with alternative words and synonyms. The resulting phrase will normally produce different connotations and prompt novel thoughts and ideas.

Second-guess technique

A technique that involves pre-empting an idea that is only partially described or revealed by the originator of that idea. In many cases, this will result in a different idea from the original one.

Index

Acknowledgements

Thank you to everyone who helped make this book possible…

First and foremost, my editor Colette Meacher of AVA Publishing, whose professionalism and expertise has helped keep this book on an even keel throughout the process.

Susannah Jayes, my picture researcher, whose energy and persistence enabled us to get all of the great images we wanted to show in this book (well most of them anyway!).

David Shaw, the designer, for making everything look so good on the page.

Thanks also to all of the industry practitioners (too many to mention individually), who have contributed directly or indirectly to this book. In particular: Simon Cenamor and Raymond Chan of HMDG, Nigel Clifton, Rachel Heathfield and Libby Clay of EHS 4D.

Special thanks to all of my colleagues and friends whose general support and friendship has helped to keep me sane through the various stages of this book, in particular: Anne Hill, Caroline Barfoot, Debbie Moores, Ken Burtenshaw, Paul Ansell and Sally Holland.

Special thanks also to all of my students at Southampton Solent University, past and present, who have inspired the content of this book.

And finally a big thank you to my family for the time I stole to write this.

BASICS

ADVERTISING

Working with ethics

Lynne Elvins
Naomi Goulder

Publisher's note

The subject of ethics is not new, yet its consideration within the applied visual arts is perhaps not as prevalent as it might be. Our aim here is to help a new generation of students, educators and practitioners find a methodology for structuring their thoughts and reflections in this vital area.

AVA Publishing hopes that these **Working with ethics** pages provide a platform for consideration and a flexible method for incorporating ethical concerns in the work of educators, students and professionals. Our approach consists of four parts:

The **introduction** is intended to be an accessible snapshot of the ethical landscape, both in terms of historical development and current dominant themes.

The **framework** positions ethical consideration into four areas and poses questions about the practical implications that might occur. Marking your response to each of these questions on the scale shown will allow your reactions to be further explored by comparison.

The **case study** sets out a real project and then poses some ethical questions for further consideration. This is a focus point for a debate rather than a critical analysis so there are no predetermined right or wrong answers.

A selection of **further reading** for you to consider areas of particular interest in more detail.

Ethical: aware-ness/ reflect-ion/ debate

Ethics is a complex subject that interlaces the idea of responsibilities to society with a wide range of considerations relevant to the character and happiness of the individual. It concerns virtues of compassion, loyalty and strength, but also of confidence, imagination, humour and optimism. As introduced in ancient Greek philosophy, the fundamental ethical question is: *what should I do?* How we might pursue a 'good' life not only raises moral concerns about the effects of our actions on others, but also personal concerns about our own integrity.

In modern times the most important and controversial questions in ethics have been the moral ones. With growing populations and improvements in mobility and communications, it is not surprising that considerations about how to structure our lives together on the planet should come to the forefront. For visual artists and communicators, it should be no surprise that these considerations will enter into the creative process.

Some ethical considerations are already enshrined in government laws and regulations or in professional codes of conduct. For example, plagiarism and breaches of confidentiality can be punishable offences. Legislation in various nations makes it unlawful to exclude people with disabilities from accessing information or spaces. The trade of ivory as a material has been banned in many countries. In these cases, a clear line has been drawn under what is unacceptable.

But most ethical matters remain open to debate, among experts and lay-people alike, and in the end we have to make our own choices on the basis of our own guiding principles or values. Is it more ethical to work for a charity than for a commercial company? Is it unethical to create something that others find ugly or offensive?

Specific questions such as these may lead to other questions that are more abstract. For example, is it only effects on humans (and what they care about) that are important, or might effects on the natural world require attention too?

Is promoting ethical consequences justified even when it requires ethical sacrifices along the way? Must there be a single unifying theory of ethics (such as the Utilitarian thesis that the right course of action is always the one that leads to the greatest happiness of the greatest number), or might there always be many different ethical values that pull a person in various directions?

As we enter into ethical debate and engage with these dilemmas on a personal and professional level, we may change our views or change our view of others. The real test though is whether, as we reflect on these matters, we change the way we act as well as the way we think. Socrates, the 'father' of philosophy, proposed that people will naturally do 'good' if they know what is right. But this point might only lead us to yet another question: *how do we know what is right?*

You
What are your ethical beliefs?

Central to everything you do will be your attitude to people and issues around you. For some people, their ethics are an active part of the decisions they make every day as a consumer, a voter or a working professional. Others may think about ethics very little and yet this does not automatically make them unethical. Personal beliefs, lifestyle, politics, nationality, religion, gender, class or education can all influence your ethical viewpoint.

Using the scale, where would you place yourself? What do you take into account to make your decision? Compare results with your friends or colleagues.

Your client
What are your terms?

Working relationships are central to whether ethics can be embedded into a project, and your conduct on a day-to-day basis is a demonstration of your professional ethics. The decision with the biggest impact is whom you choose to work with in the first place. Cigarette companies or arms traders are often-cited examples when talking about where a line might be drawn, but rarely are real situations so extreme. At what point might you turn down a project on ethical grounds and how much does the reality of having to earn a living affect your ability to choose?

Using the scale, where would you place a project? How does this compare to your personal ethical level?

01 02 03 04 05 06 07 08 09 10

01 02 03 04 05 06 07 08 09 10

Your specifications
What are the impacts of your materials?

In relatively recent times, we are learning that many natural materials are in short supply. At the same time, we are increasingly aware that some man-made materials can have harmful, long-term effects on people or the planet. How much do you know about the materials that you use? Do you know where they come from, how far they travel and under what conditions they are obtained? When your creation is no longer needed, will it be easy and safe to recycle? Will it disappear without a trace? Are these considerations your responsibility or are they out of your hands?

Using the scale, mark how ethical your material choices are.

Your creation
What is the purpose of your work?

Between you, your colleagues and an agreed brief, what will your creation achieve? What purpose will it have in society and will it make a positive contribution? Should your work result in more than commercial success or industry awards? Might your creation help save lives, educate, protect or inspire? Form and function are two established aspects of judging a creation, but there is little consensus on the obligations of visual artists and communicators toward society, or the role they might have in solving social or environmental problems. If you want recognition for being the creator, how responsible are you for what you create and where might that responsibility end?

Using the scale, mark how ethical the purpose of your work is.

01 02 03 04 05 06 07 08 09 10

01 02 03 04 05 06 07 08 09 10

One aspect of advertising that raises an ethical dilemma is the use of gender stereotypes. The repeated use of stereotypes impacts on how children associate genders with certain traits and how they then form positive or negative views of themselves and other people. Stereotypes often reflect deeply embedded prejudices within cultures and play a significant role in shaping the attitudes of people in that culture. Portrayals of adult women in American television have been found to emphasize passivity and lack of intelligence whereas men have been portrayed as constructive and achieving. Similarly, analysis of print advertising indicated that women were often depicted as shy, gentle and helpless whereas men's body language denoted power, control and dominance.

When a character is presented as a stereotype, he or she is given a relatively fixed, unalterable and predictable image. But stereotypes also provide a way to communicate an instantly recognizable set of values or aspirations and, as such, can be valuable tools for the advertiser to work with. Is it the responsibility of advertisers to break from stereotypes in order to shift cultures away from prejudice?

Subliminal messages are small pieces of embedded information that are undetected by the viewer or listener. They achieve this by passing below the normal limits of perception. Communicating with the subconscious mind in this way is believed to be able to negatively or positively influence subsequent thoughts, behaviours, actions, attitudes, beliefs or value systems.

Trained in social psychology at the University of Michigan, James McDonald Vicary pioneered the use of eye-blink analysis to measure levels of emotional tension when people were exposed to various stimuli. In his experiment, people watching a film at a New Jersey cinema were repeatedly and unknowingly flashed the words 'eat popcorn' and 'drink Coca-Cola' for about 1/300th of a second on the screen. The result was that sales of popcorn and Coca-Cola are said to have increased dramatically. Vicary's work led him to coin the term 'subliminal advertising'.

Newsday called subliminal stimulation 'the most alarming invention since the atomic bomb'. A public outcry developed and the practice of subliminal advertising was banned in the US, UK and Australia. But in spite of the popular belief that subliminal messages were widely used, there was arguably little evidence to support it.

No detailed study of Vicary's findings was ever released and no independent evidence turned up to support his claim. Eventually, in 1962 for an *Advertising Age* interview, Vicary admitted that the original study was a fabricated 'gimmick'.

But further claims in the 1970s that subliminal techniques were still widely used raised public fears once again. Wilson Bryan Key, author of *Subliminal Seduction*, said that he had found 13 advertising firms that were prepared to produce subliminal messages for advertisers. This refuelled public concern enough that The Federal Communications Commission (FCC) held hearings in 1974 and declared that subliminal advertising was 'contrary to the public interest' because it involved 'intentional deception'.

To commemorate its 50th anniversary, the Vicary experiment was replicated at the International Branding Conference, MARKA 2007. The 1,400 delegates watched part of the movie used in the original experiment and were then asked to choose between two fictitious brands, one of which had been subliminally cut into the footage. When choosing between the two brands, 81 per cent of the audience chose the one that had been used, suggesting evidence of Vicary's results.

Is subliminal advertising unethical?

If a subliminal message encouraged people to 'eat healthier' or 'be kind', would that make it more ethical?

Would you knowingly insert a subliminal message into a piece of advertising?

Good advertising does not just circulate information. It penetrates the public mind with desires and belief.
Leo Burnett

AIGA
Design Business and Ethics
2007, AIGA

Eaton, Marcia Muelder
Aesthetics and the Good Life
1989, Associated University Press

Ellison, David
Ethics and Aesthetics in European Modernist Literature:
From the Sublime to the Uncanny
2001, Cambridge University Press

Fenner, David E W (Ed)
Ethics and the Arts:
An Anthology
1995, Garland Reference Library of Social Science

Gini, Al and Marcoux, Alexei M
Case Studies in Business Ethics
2005, Prentice Hall

McDonough, William and Braungart, Michael
Cradle to Cradle:
Remaking the Way We Make Things
2002, North Point Press

Papanek, Victor
Design for the Real World:
Making to Measure
1972, Thames & Hudson

United Nations Global Compact
The Ten Principles
www.unglobalcompact.org/AboutTheGC/TheTenPrinciples/index.html